Cold Intimacies

To Elchanan

Cold Intimacies: The Making of Emotional Capitalism

EVA ILLOUZ

polity

First published in 2007 by Polity Press

Polity Press
65 Bridge Street
Cambridge CB2 1UR, UK.

Polity Press
350 Main Street
Malden, MA 02148, USA

ISBN-10: 0-7456-3904-6
ISBN-13: 978-07456-3904-8
ISBN-10: 0-7456-3905-4 (pb)
ISBN-13: 978-07456-3905-5 (pb)

A catalogue record for this book is available from the British Library.

Typeset in 11 on 13 pt Scala
by SNP Best-set Typesetter Ltd, Hong Kong
Printed and bound in Malaysia by Alden Press, Malaysia.

The publisher has done its best to ensure that the URLs for external websites
referred to in this book are correct and active at the time of going to press.
However, the publisher has no responsibility for the websites and can make no
guarantee that a site will remain live or that the content is or will remain
appropriate.

Every effort has been made to trace all copyright holders, but if any has been
inadvertently overlooked, the publishers will be pleased to include any necessary
credits in any subsequent reprint or edition.

For further information on Polity, visit our website: www.polity.co.uk

Contents

Acknowledgments

Few books owe their existence to the initiative of a single person. This book is one of them. When he invited me to deliver the Adorno Lectures in Frankfurt, Axel Honneth compelled me to stop and think again about what I was working on at the time, namely the role of psychology in shaping the ordinary cultural frames of middle-class men and women in much of the contemporary world. I re-read critical theorists, and came to realize with a renewed acuity that the long tradition of critical theory starting, from Theodor Adorno to Axel Honneth via Habermas, has yet to be surpassed in its capacity to make sense of the conflicting tendencies at work in modernity. Axel's towering intellectual vision, his generosity and relentless energy stand squarely behind the making of this book.

I thank wholeheartedly Viviana Zelizer for having made possible a visiting position at the department of Sociology at Princeton University during which I wrote these lectures. My deep gratitude goes to the cheerful and efficient librarians of the Institute for Advanced Study.

Beatrice Smedley read all three chapters, and with her exceptional kindness and sharpness offered a lot to reflect about and to improve on. Carol Kidron's own work on trauma as well as her critical insights contributed to the book. Eitan Wilf must be thanked for reading the manuscript and offering, with his usual directness, sharp criticisms and judicious bibliographical additions. Lior Flum has been an invaluable help in the sometimes difficult process of making a book presentable.

I thank wholeheartedly Sarah Dancy, Emma Hutchinson, and Gail Ferguson at Polity Press for their thoroughness, professionalism, and kindness.

Finally, I dedicate this book to my husband and best friend, Elchanan, who did more than his share of reading, criticizing, discussing the book, spent a considerable amount of his time listening to many confused hesitations, and shared in more than a few moments of unthinking happiness.

Eva Illouz

1 The Rise of *Homo Sentimentalis*

Sociologists have traditionally conceived of modernity in terms of the advent of capitalism, the rise of democratic political institutions, or the moral force of the idea of individualism, but have taken little notice of the fact that, along with the familiar concepts of surplus value, exploitation, rationalization, disenchantment, or division of labor, most grand sociological accounts of modernity contained, in a minor key, another story: namely descriptions or accounts of the advent of modernity in terms of emotions. To take a few glaring yet seemingly trivial examples, Weber's Protestant ethic contains at its core a thesis about the role of emotions in economic action, for it is the anxiety provoked by an inscrutable divinity which is at the heart of the capitalist entrepreneur's frantic activity.[1] Marx's alienation – which was central in explaining the worker's relation to the process and product of labor – had strong emotional overtones, as when Marx, in *The Economic and Philosophic Manuscripts*, discusses alienated labor as a loss of reality, in his words, a loss of the bond to the object.[2] When Marx's "alienation" was appropriated – and distorted – by popular culture, it was mostly for its emotional implications: modernity and capitalism were alienating in the sense that they created a form of emotional numbness which separated people from one another, from their community, and from their own deep selves. Or still we may evoke Simmel's famous depiction of Metropolis which contains an account of emotional life. For Simmel, urban life creates an endless flow of nervous stimulations and stands in contrast to small-town life which rests on emotional relationships. The typically modern attitude, for Simmel, is that of the "blasé," a mix of reserve, coldness and indifference, and, Simmel adds, always in danger of turning into hatred.[3] Finally, Durkheim's sociology is – perhaps surprisingly for the neo-Kantian that he was – most obviously concerned with emotions. Indeed, "solidarity," the linchpin of Durkheim's sociology, is nothing but a bundle of emotions binding social actors to the central symbols of society (what Durkheim called "effervescence" in the *Elementary Forms of Religious Life*).[4] (In the conclusion of *Symbolic Classifications*,[5] Durkheim and Mauss claim that symbolic classifications – cognitive entities *par excellence* – have an emotional core.) Durkheim's view of modernity was even more directly concerned with emotions as he tried to understand how, given that the social differentiation of modern societies lacked emotional intensity, modern society still "held together."[6]

My point is clear enough, and I do not need to belabor it: unbeknown to them, canonical sociological accounts of modernity contain, if not a full-fledged theory of emotions, at least numerous references to them: anxiety, love, competitiveness, indifference, guilt are all present in most historical and sociological accounts of the ruptures which have led to the modern era, if we only care to scratch its surface.[7] My broad claim in this book is that when we recover that not-so-hidden dimension of modernity, standard analyses of what constitutes modern selfhood and identity, of the private–public divide and its articulation on gender divisions, become seriously altered.

But, you may ask, why should we do that? Wouldn't focusing on such a highly subjective, invisible, and personal experience as "emotion" undercut the vocation of sociology, which has been, after all, chiefly concerned with objective regularities, patterned action, and large-scale institutions? Why, in other words, should we fuss and mess with a category without which sociology has done, thus far, quite well? There are, I think, quite a few reasons.[8/9]

Emotion is *not* action per se, but it is the inner energy that propels us toward an act, what gives a particular "mood" or "coloration" to an act. Emotion can thus be defined as the "energy-laden" side of action, where that energy is understood to simultaneously implicate cognition, affect, evaluation, motivation, and the body.[10/11] Far from being pre-social or pre-cultural, emotions are cultural meanings and social relationships that are inseparably compressed together and it is this compression which confers on them their capacity to energize action. (What makes emotion carry this "energy" is the fact that it always concerns the self and the relationship of the self to culturally situated others.) When you tell me "you are late again," whether I feel shame, anger, or guilt will depend almost exclusively on my relationship to you. My boss's remark about my being late is likely to shame me, a colleague's is likely to make me angry, but if it is my child waiting for me at school, it is likely to make me feel guilty. Emotion is certainly a psychological entity, but it is no less and perhaps more so a cultural and social one: through emotion we enact cultural definitions of personhood as they are expressed in concrete and immediate but always culturally and socially defined relationships. I would thus say that emotions are cultural meanings and social relationships that are very compressed together and that it is this compact compression which confers on them their energetic and hence their pre-reflexive, often semi-conscious character. Emotions are deeply internalized and unreflexive aspects of action, but not because they do not contain enough culture and society in them, but rather because they have too much.

For this reason, a hermeneutic sociology which wants to understand social action from "within" cannot do that adequately without paying attention to the emotional coloration of action and to what actually propels it.

Emotions have another cardinal importance for sociology: much of social arrangements are also emotional arrangements. It is trivial to say that the most fundamental division and distinction organizing most societies around the world – that between men and women – is based on (and reproduces itself through) emotional cultures.[12] To be a man of character requires one to display courage, cool-headed rationality, and disciplined aggressiveness. Femininity on the other hand demands kindness, compassion, and cheerfulness. (The social hierarchy produced by gender divisions contains implicit emotional divisions, without which men and women would not reproduce their roles and identities.) And these divisions in turn produce emotional hierarchies, whereby cool-headed rationality is usually deemed more reliable, objective, and professional than, say, compassion. For example, the ideal of objectivity which dominates our conception of the news or of (blind) justice, presupposes such male practice and model of emotional self-control. Emotions are thus organized hierarchically and this type of emotional hierarchy in turn implicitly organizes moral and social arrangements.

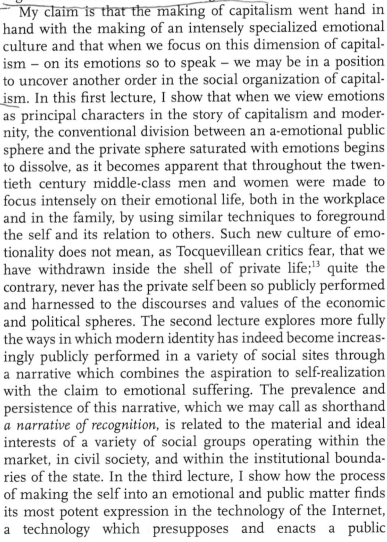

My claim is that the making of capitalism went hand in hand with the making of an intensely specialized emotional culture and that when we focus on this dimension of capitalism – on its emotions so to speak – we may be in a position to uncover another order in the social organization of capitalism. In this first lecture, I show that when we view emotions as principal characters in the story of capitalism and modernity, the conventional division between an a-emotional public sphere and the private sphere saturated with emotions begins to dissolve, as it becomes apparent that throughout the twentieth century middle-class men and women were made to focus intensely on their emotional life, both in the workplace and in the family, by using similar techniques to foreground the self and its relation to others. Such new culture of emotionality does not mean, as Tocquevillean critics fear, that we have withdrawn inside the shell of private life;[13] quite the contrary, never has the private self been so publicly performed and harnessed to the discourses and values of the economic and political spheres. The second lecture explores more fully the ways in which modern identity has indeed become increasingly publicly performed in a variety of social sites through a narrative which combines the aspiration to self-realization with the claim to emotional suffering. The prevalence and persistence of this narrative, which we may call as shorthand *a narrative of recognition*, is related to the material and ideal interests of a variety of social groups operating within the market, in civil society, and within the institutional boundaries of the state. In the third lecture, I show how the process of making the self into an emotional and public matter finds its most potent expression in the technology of the Internet, a technology which presupposes and enacts a public emotional self and in fact even makes the public emotional self precede private interactions and constitute them.

Although each lecture can be read separately, there is an organic link between them and a cumulative progression toward the main goal of these three lectures, namely to draw the contours of what I call *emotional capitalism*. Emotional capitalism is a culture in which emotional and economic discourses and practices mutually shape each other, thus producing what I view as a broad, sweeping movement in which affect is made an essential aspect of economic behavior and in which emotional life – especially that of the middle classes – follows the logic of economic relations and exchange. Inevitably, the themes of "rationalization" and "commodification" (of emotions) are recurrent topics running throughout all three lectures. Yet, my analysis is neither Marxian nor Weberian in that I do not presuppose that economy and emotions can be (or ought to be) separate from each other.[14] In fact, as I show, market-based cultural repertoires shape and inform interpersonal and emotional relationships, while interpersonal relationships are at the epicenter of economic relationships. More exactly, market repertoires become intertwined with the language of psychology and, combined together, offer new techniques and meanings to forge new forms of sociability. In the following section, I will examine how this new mode of sociability emerged and what are its core emotional (imaginary) significations.

Freud and the Clark lectures

If I had to forget my training as a cultural sociologist as well as my deep-seated suspicion of assignable dates to major cultural shifts, and if I was nonetheless forced to choose a date which marked the transformation of American emotional culture, I would pick 1909, the year Sigmund Freud went to lecture in America at Clark University. In five broad-sweeping lectures, Freud presented, before an eclectic audience, the major ideas of psychoanalysis, or at any rate those ideas which would find a resounding echo in American popular culture, such as slips of the tongue, the role of the unconscious in determining our destiny, the centrality of dreams for psychic life, the sexual character of most of our desires, the family as the origin of our psyche and ultimate cause of its pathologies. It is rather strange that many sociological and historical analyses have offered us elaborate and sophisticated accounts of psychoanalysis in terms of its intellectual origins,[15] or its impact on cultural conceptions of the self, or in terms of its relationship to scientific ideas, but have overlooked a simple and glaring fact, namely that psychoanalysis and the wide variety of dissident theories of the psyche which followed had, by and large, the primary vocation of reshaping emotional life (although of course it seemed to be merely interested in dissecting it). More exactly, the many and various strands of clinical psychology – Freudian, Ego psychology, Humanist, Object-Relation – formulated what I suggest calling a new emotional style – the therapeutic emotional style – which has dominated the American cultural landscape throughout the twentieth century.

What is an "emotional style"? In her well-known *Philosophy in a New Key*, Susanne Langer suggests that every age in the history of philosophy "has its own preoccupation . . ." and that "it is the mode of handling problems" – what Langer calls their "technique" – rather than what they are about "that assigns them to an age."[16] I use the term therapeutic emotional style for the ways in which twentieth-century culture became "preoccupied" with emotional life – its etiology and morphology – and devised specific "techniques" – linguistic, scientific, interactional – to apprehend and manage these emotions.[17] Modern emotional style has been shaped mostly (albeit not exclusively) by the language of therapy which emerged in a relatively short period running from the First World War to the Second World War. If, as Jürgen Habermas put it, "The end of the nineteenth century saw a discipline emerge [psychoanalysis], primarily as the work of a single man . . . [Freud],"[18] I would add that this discipline quickly became more than a discipline, that is, a specialized body of knowledge. It was a new set of cultural practices which, because they were in the unique position of being located in the realm of scientific production as well as in the twin realms of elite and popular cultures, reorganized conceptions of self, emotional life, and even social relations. Recalling Robert Bellah's expression about the Protestant Reformation, we may say that the therapeutic discourse has "reformulated the deepest level of identity symbols,"[19] and it is through such identity symbols that the reformulation of a new emotional style took place.

An emotional style takes place when a new interpersonal imagination is formulated, that is, a new way of thinking about the relationship of self to others and imagining its potentialities. Indeed, interpersonal relationships – like the nation – are thought of, longed for, argued over, betrayed, fought for, and negotiated according to imaginary scripts which fill social closeness or distance with meaning.[20] Thus, I would argue that Freud's greatest impact on culture has been to reformulate *the relationship of the self* and its relationship to others through a new way of imagining the position of the self vis-à-vis one's past. Such interpersonal imagination was formulated in a number of key ideas and cultural motives which would haunt American popular culture.

First, in the psychoanalytical imagination, the nuclear family is the very point of origin of the self – the site within which and from which the story and history of the self could begin. Where the family had hitherto been a way of "objectively" situating oneself in a long chronological chain and in the social order, it now became a biographical event symbolically carried throughout one's life and uniquely expressing one's individuality. Ironically, at the same time that the traditional foundations of marriage started to crumble, the family came back to haunt the self with a vengeance, but this time as a "story" and as a way to "emplot" the self. The family played a role that was all the more crucial for the constitution of new narratives of selfhood in that it was both the very origin of the self and that which the self had to be liberated from.

Second, the new psychoanalytical imagination firmly located the self within the realm of everyday life, a realm dubbed by Stanley Cavell as that of the "uneventful."[21] For example, the *Psychopathology of Everyday Life*,[22] which had been published in 1901 and whose ideas permeated the Clark lectures, claimed to inaugurate a new science on the basis of the most banal and unspectacular occurrences, namely parapraxes, slips of the tongue, which, Freud tells us, are in fact the repository of highly significant meaning regarding our self and its deepest desires. Freud's theory of the self was part and parcel of the bourgeois cultural revolution which moved away from contemplative or heroic definitions of identity and situated it in the realm of everyday life, chiefly in the workplace and in the family.[23] But the Freudian imagination went one step further: it now bestowed on the ordinary self a new glamour, as it was awaiting to be discovered and fashioned. The ordinary, mundane self became mysterious, difficult to achieve. As Peter Gay suggests in his biographical and philosophical portrait of Freud, "What everyone is used to calling 'normal' in sexual conduct is really the end point of a long, often interrupted, pilgrimage, a goal that many humans may never reach. The sexual drive in its mature – normal – form is *an achievement*"[24] (emphasis added). What made the mundane self an enticing object of imagination was the fact that it now synthesized two opposing cultural images: that of normality and that of pathology. Freud's extraordinary cultural achievement consisted both in enlarging the scope of the normal by incorporating in it what was hitherto defined as pathological (for example his idea that sexual development starts with homosexuality), and in problematizing normality, thus making it an arduous goal which, for it to be reached, now demanded the mobilization of a large array of cultural resources (for example, heterosexuality was not a given any more but rather it became a goal to achieve). Thus, if, as Foucault has claimed, the nineteenth-century psychiatric discourse instituted a rigid boundary between the normal and the pathological,[25] Freud systematically blurred that boundary and posited a new kind of normality, riddled with a new cast of pathological characters, an open-ended project for the self, an undefined and yet powerful goal for the self.

Last but far from least, Freud put at the epicenter of this new imagination sex, sexual pleasure, and sexuality. Given the large amount of cultural resources that had been mobilized to regulate sexuality, it seems fairly reasonable to argue that an open-ended project of the self in which sex and sexuality appeared as the powerful unconscious causes of pathologies, and which also was the sign of mature and complete development, could only fire the censored imagination of Freud's contemporaries. What allowed sexuality to be so smoothly incorporated into the modern imagination was the fact that it was combined with another supremely modern motive, namely language, thus moving away from the nineteenth-century "primitivist" connotations of sexuality. Not only was language saturated with new and unsuspected sexuality (as for example in the theme of "parapraxes," or slips of the tongue), but sexuality itself became now a chiefly linguistic affair, something to be achieved after a considerable amount of conceptual clarification and verbalization.

There are many institutional and organizational reasons for the extraordinary success of the psychoanalytical imagination in the US. The increasingly triangular structure of the American family, dubbed by John Demos the "hothouse" family, entertained a close affinity with the Freudian triangular theory of the Oedipus complex;[26] Freud's theories resonated with the quest for authenticity that was at the epicenter of the nascent and intensive consumer culture;[27] Freud's theories were received and diffused by various members of the academic, medical and literary establishment;[28] the institutional boundaries between medicine and popular culture were thin, thus making doctors into popularizers of new ideas such as Freudianism;[29] finally, there was a fierce debate between scientific medicine and spiritual medicine, and the Freudian paradigm seemed to reconcile the two.[30] Unfortunately I cannot dwell on the intricate reasons why Freud's ideas caught fire within American institutions. Let me simply say that because psychoanalysis was in the unique position of bridging the specialized practices of psychology, neurology, psychiatry, and medicine on the one hand and high and low cultures on the other, it could spread widely in all venues for American culture, most conspicuously in the movies and in advice literature.

In the 1920s, advice literature was, like the movies, an emerging cultural industry, and it would prove to be the most enduring platform for the diffusion of psychological ideas and for the elaboration of emotional norms. Advice literature combines a number of exigencies: it must be, by definition, general in character, that is, use a law-like language that confers on it authority and enables it to make law-like statements; it must vary the problems it addresses for it to be a commodity consumed on a regular basis; moreover, if it wants to address various segments of readership, with differing values and viewpoints, it must be amoral, that is, offer a neutral perspective on problems having to do with sexuality and the conduct of social relationships. Finally, it must be credible, that is, be proffered by a legitimate source. Psychoanalysis and psychology were goldmines for the advice industry because they were wrapped in the aura of science, because they could be highly individualized (fitting any and all individual particularity), because they could address a wide variety of problems, thereby enabling product diversification, and because they seemed to offer the dispassionate gaze of science on tabooed topics. With the expanding consumer market, the book industry and women's magazines avidly seized upon a language which could accommodate both theory and story, generality and particularity, non-judgmentality and normativity. While advice literature does not have a straightforward impact on its readers, its importance in providing a vocabulary for the self and for negotiating social relations has been insufficiently acknowledged. Much of contemporary cultural material comes to us in the form of advice, admonition, and how-to recipes, and given that in many social sites the modern self is self-made – drawing upon various cultural repertoires to decide on a course of action – advice literature is likely to have played an important role in shaping the vocabularies through which the self understands itself.

Reshaping the corporate imagination

Psychologists differed from other experts and professionals (such as lawyers or engineers) in that they slowly but surely claimed expertise in virtually all areas – from the military to childrearing via marketing and sexuality[31] – and used advice literature to ascertain such vocation. As the twentieth century unfolded, they increasingly assumed the vocation of guiding others on a variety of problems in the fields of education, criminal behavior, legal expert testimony, marriage, prison rehabilitation programs, sexuality, racial and political conflict, economic behavior, and soldiers' morale.[32]

Nowhere was this influence more palpable than in the American corporation, where psychologists intertwined emotions with the realm of economic action in the form of a radically new way of conceiving of production. The period running from the 1880s to the 1920s has been dubbed the golden age of capitalism, during which "the factory system was established, capital was centralized, production standardized, organizations bureaucratized, and labor incorporated in large firms."[33] Most conspicuous was the rise of the large-scale corporation, employing thousands and sometimes even tens of thousands of workers, thus "making corporations bureaucratically complex and hierarchically integrated."[34] By the 1920s, 86 percent of all wage-earners were employed in manufacturing.[35] Even more conspicuous was the fact that the American firm had the largest proportion of administrative workers worldwide (18 administrative workers for each 100 production workers).[36] The expansion of firms went hand in hand with the consolidation of management theories which aimed to systematize and rationalize the production process. Indeed, the management system shifted – or rather multiplied – the loci of control, which now moved from the hands of traditional capitalists to those of technocrats who used the rhetoric of science, rationality, and general welfare to establish their authority. Some view this transformation as the seizure of a new form of power by engineers who acted as a class of professionals who imposed a new ideology – of management – which conceived of the workplace as a "system," in which the individual would be eradicated and where general rules and laws would be formalized and applied to the worker and to the work process.[37] In contrast to capitalists, who had frequently been portrayed as greedy and selfish, in the new ideology of management, the manager emerged as rational, responsible, and predictable, and as the bearer of new rules of standardization and rationalization.[38] Engineers tended to think of men as machines, and of the corporation as an impersonal system to operate. But this view overlooks an important fact, namely that in parallel to the engineers' rhetoric or in its aftermath another discourse emerged, spearheaded by psychologists, which paid a great deal of attention to the individual, to the irrational dimension of work relationships, and to workers' emotions.[39]

From the beginning of the twentieth century, experimental psychologists were solicited by managers to find solutions to the problem of discipline and productivity inside the corporation.[40] Around the 1920s, it was clinical psychologists, many of whom were inspired by Freudian psychodynamic views and who had been particularly successful in the army in helping recruit soldiers or heal war traumas, who were mobilized by the corporation to help formulate needed guidelines for the new task of management.

Elton Mayo must be given a place of honor in any account of management theory because "there can be few disciplines or fields of research in which a single set of studies or single researcher and writer has exercised so great an influence as was exercised for a quarter of the century by Mayo and the Hawthorne studies."[41] Where experimental psychologists who had preceded the human relations movement had claimed that moral qualities such as "loyalty" or "reliability" were crucial attributes of the productive personality inside a corporation, Mayo's famous Hawthorne experiments – conducted from 1924 to 1927 – paid historically unprecedented attention to emotional transactions per se as his main finding was that productivity increased if work relationships contained care and attention to workers' feelings. In place of the Victorian moral language of "character," Mayo, who had been trained as a Jungian psychoanalyst, introduced the psychoanalytical imagination inside the workplace.[42] Mayo's intervention in the corporation had a thoroughly therapeutic character. For example, the method of interview Mayo set up had *all* the characteristics (except the name) of a therapeutic interview. This is in fact how Mayo presents his method of interviewing to the disgruntled workers of the plant at General Electric where he and his team intervened:

Workers wished to talk, and to talk freely, under the seal of professional confidence (which was never abused) to someone who
seemed representative of the company or who seemed, by his very
attitude, to carry authority. The experience itself was unusual;
there are few people in this world who have had the experience
of finding someone intelligent, attentive, and eager to listen
without interruption to all that he or she has to say. But to arrive
at this point it became necessary to train interviewers how to
listen, how to avoid interruption or the giving of advice, how
generally to avoid anything that might put an end to free expression in an individual instance. Some approximate rules to guide
the interviewer in his work were therefore set down. These were,
more or less, as follows:

1　Give your whole attention to the person interviewed, and
　　make it evident that you are doing so.
2　Listen – don't talk.
3　Never argue; never give advice.
4　Listen to:
　　(a)　what he wants to say
　　(b)　what he does not want to say
　　(c)　what he cannot say without help
5　As you listen, plot out tentatively and for subsequent correc-
　　tion the pattern (personal) that is being set before you. To test
　　this, from time to time summarize what has been said and
　　present for comment (e.g., "is this what you are telling me?").
　　Always do this with the greatest caution, that is, clarify in
　　ways that do not add or distort.
6　Remember that everything said must be considered a per-
　　sonal confidence and not divulged to anyone.[43]

I personally do not know of a better definition of the therapeutic interview, which precisely aims at eliciting uncensored
speech and emotions and at building trust. Mayo seemed to
stumble accidentally on the importance of emotions, family,
and close bonds, but he was in fact only importing therapeutic
categories into the workplace. An analysis of the original cases
addressed by Mayo is instructive both of the ways in which his
approach to work conflicts was shaped by psychological
methods, and of the ways in which his method elicited

emotional talk and evoked the specter of the family inside the workplace. The problems he unraveled among women workers were framed as having an emotional nature and as mirroring their family history: for example, "one woman worker . . . discovered during an interview that her dislike of a certain supervisor was based upon a fancied resemblance to a detested stepfather. Small wonder that the same supervisor had warned the interviewer that she was 'difficult to handle.' "[44] Or to give another example, the interviewer was able to establish that a woman's performance was suffering because her mother had pressured her to ask for a raise:

> She talked her situation out with an interviewer, and it became clear that to her a raise would mean separation from her daily companions and associates. Although not immediately relevant, it is interesting to note that, after explaining the situation to the interviewer, she was able to present her case dispassionately to her mother . . . the mother immediately understood and abandoned pressure for advancement, and the girl returned to work. This last instance illustrates one way in which the interview opens emotional blockage in lines of communication – within as well as without the plant.[45]

Notice how family ties are naturally brought into the workplace and how, in the latter example, the expression "emotional blockage" puts affect and the psychoanalytical imagination right at the center of work relationships and productivity. The language of emotionality and that of productive efficiency were becoming increasingly intertwined, each shaping the other.

Elton Mayo revolutionized management theories because, at the same time that he recast the moral language of selfhood into the dispassionate terminology of psychological science, he substituted a new lexicon of "human relations" for the engineers' rhetoric of rationality that had hitherto prevailed. By suggesting that conflicts were not a matter of competition over scarce resources but rather resulted from tangled emotions, personality factors, and unresolved psychological conflicts, Mayo established a discursive *continuity between the family and*

the workplace and in fact introduced the psychoanalytical imagination at the very heart of the language of economic efficiency. More than that: being a good manager increasingly
meant displaying the attributes of a good psychologist: it
required being able to grasp, listen to, and deal dispassionately
with the complex emotional nature of social transactions in
the workplace. For example, when workers voiced grievances,
Mayo and his team recommended that a manager ought to
listen to their anger, which, Mayo suggested, would in fact
help calm them down.[46]

But what is perhaps even more interesting is the fact that
in Mayo's experiments at General Electric, the subjects were
all women and that, unbeknownst to himself, Mayo's findings
were highly gendered: thus if, as many feminists have claimed,
masculinity is implicitly inscribed in most of our cultural categories, surely Mayo's findings are an example of the reverse,
namely the inscription of femininity in "universal" claims.
Mayo used a female method – based on speech and the communication of emotions – to unravel the problems of his
women subjects inside the American corporation, that is, problems which had a fundamentally interpersonal and emotional
nature. For example, Mayo claimed that after his team of
researchers talked to the workers, productivity increased
because, he hypothesized, the workers had felt important and
singled out, had developed good interpersonal relationships,
and had had relationships with one another which had made
for a much more pleasant working environment. Mayo was
applying the conceptual tools of psychology to women, and
based on his findings, he and the cohort of organizational
consultants who would work in his footsteps inadvertently
initiated a process in which aspects of women's emotional
experiences and selfhood were incorporated into the new
guidelines to manage human relationships in the modern
workplace. In so doing, Mayo had thus also made a significant
contribution to the process of redefining masculinity inside
the workplace.

More: the new approach to emotions *softened the character
of the foreman.* Indeed as social historian Stephanie Coontz
notices: "The qualities men . . . needed to work in industrial

America were almost feminine ones: tact, teamwork, the ability to accept direction. New definitions of masculinity had to be constructed that did not derive directly from the work process."[47] From the 1920s onward, under the impetus of new management theory, managers had to revise, unknowingly, traditional definitions of masculinity and incorporate in their personality so-called feminine attributes – such as paying attention to emotions, controlling anger, and listening sympathetically to others. This new type of masculinity was not without contradictions, as it was supposed to ward off attributes of femininity, yet it was also closer to feminine self-conscious attention to one's own and others' emotions than had ever been the case in industrial work plants.

Thus, whereas Victorian emotional culture had divided men and women through the axis of the public and private spheres, the twentieth-century therapeutic culture slowly eroded and reshuffled these boundaries by making emotional life central to the workplace.

A new emotional style

The language of psychology was enormously successful in shaping the discourse of corporate selfhood because it was able to make sense of the transformations of the capitalist workplace and because it naturalized new forms of competition and hierarchies, all of which were extrinsic to the psychological persuasion per se but which were increasingly codified by it. As corporations grew larger and created greater layers of managers between employees and upper management and as American society became oriented toward a service economy – on its way to the so-called post-industrial society – a scientific discourse that dealt primarily with persons, interactions, and emotions was the natural candidate to shape the language of selfhood in the workplace. The psychological discourse was enormously successful because in the background of the rise of the professions,[48] psychologists offered a language – of persons, emotions, motivations – which seemed to correspond to and make sense of the large-scale transformations of the

American workplace. As Karl Mannheim put it in his classic study on *Ideology and Utopia*: "*[a] style of thought [is] an endless series of responses to certain typical situations characterizing their common position.*"[49] Because corporate hierarchy began demanding an orientation to persons as well as to commodities and because the corporation demanded coordination and cooperation, the management of self in the workplace increasingly became a "problem." With the recession and the steep rise in unemployment rates that accompanied it in the late 1920s, work was becoming more uncertain.[50] Uncertainty in turn bred reliance on expert theories. Psychologists acted as "knowledge specialists" who developed ideas and methods to improve human relations, and who thereby transformed the "structure of knowledge" or consciousness that shaped the thinking of laypersons. Moreover, for managers and corporation owners, the language of psychology was particularly well suited to their interests: psychologists seemed to promise nothing less than to increase profits, fight labor unrest, organize manager–worker relationships in a non-confrontational way, and neutralize class struggles by casting them in the benign language of emotions and personality. On the workers' part, the language of psychology was attractive because it had the appearance of being more democratic, for it now made good leadership depend on personality and on the capacity to understand others rather than on innate privilege and social standing. After all, in the previous system of control over the workers, the "workers had to submit to the authority of foremen in issues such as hiring, firing, pay, promotion, and workload. Most foremen used a 'drive system,' a method involving strict supervision and verbal abuse."[51] While most sociologists have viewed the early uses of psychology inside the corporation as a new form of subtle and, hence, more powerful control, I beg to differ and suggest instead that it carried a significant appeal for the workers because it democratized the power-ridden relations between workers and managers and instilled the new belief that one's personality – independent of social status – was the key to social and managerial success. Thus the discourse of psychology engineered a new form of sociability and emotionality at the basis of which were two key cultural motives: that of "equality" and that of "cooperation," for relationships were forged between people who were presumed to be equals; and the goal of these relationships was to cooperate in order to make work more efficient. The twin assumptions of equality and cooperation now exerted new constraints on the conduct of social relationships inside the corporation, constraints which cannot be equated with "false consciousness," "surveillance," or "ideology."

The communicative ethic as the spirit of the corporation

Psychologists created new models of behavior by creating new objects of analysis which in turn mobilized a wide array of instruments, practices, and institutions. The different theories that were elaborated by popular psychologists writing guidebooks on management from the 1930s to the 1970s converged around one leading cultural model: that of "communication." Sociologists are so accustomed to associating "communication" with Habermas that they have forgotten that the idea and cultural ideal of communication has been in circulation in the literature on management and in popular culture for the last three or four decades. The therapeutic idea of "communication" came to designate the emotional, linguistic, and ultimately personal attributes required to be a good manager and a competent member of a corporation. The notion of "communication" – and of what I would like to almost call "communicative competence" – is an outstanding example of what Foucault called an episteme, a new object of knowledge which in turn generates new instruments and practices of knowledge.[52] But Foucault did not – and given his theoretical premises perhaps could not – inquire about what people actually *do* with certain forms of knowledge, what they are "good for" in concrete social relationships. That is, in contrast to Foucaultian approaches which lump together psychological meanings and practices under the heading of "discipline," "surveillance," and "governmentality," I suggest we operate a pragmatic move,[53] that is, that we inquire about what people actually do with knowledge, how they produce meanings that "work" in different contexts and social spheres.[54]

The linguistic model of communication is a cultural tool and repertoire used as a way to help coordinate actors *between and within* themselves – i.e., to coordinate relations between people presumed equals and entitled to the same rights – and to coordinate the complex cognitive and emotional apparatus required to do that. "Communication" is thus a technology of self-management relying extensively on language and on the proper management of emotions but with the aim of engineering inter- and intra-emotional coordination.

According to the imperative of communication put forth by popular psychology, the first imperative of a good manager is to evaluate oneself "objectively," which means to understand how one appears to others, which in turn means to engage in a fairly complex work of introspection. Numerous guidebooks on successful leadership prescribe that one become a Meadian actor, evaluating and comparing one's self-image with the image others have of oneself. As an advice book puts it: "Without the management training course [a communication workshop], Mike's career might well have remained stagnant, not because he lacks ability but because he *didn't understand that he was giving other people the wrong impression of himself.*"[55] The advice literature on successful management conditioned success on one's capacity to see oneself from the outside, so to speak, in order to control one's impact on others. However, this new dexterity with one's appearance was not to invite a cold or cynical approach to others. Quite the opposite: the Meadian-like reflexive selfhood is commanded to develop skills of sympathy and empathy. For example, in 1937, inside the immensely popular book *How to Win Friends and Influence People*, Dale Carnegie wrote: "If as a result of reading this book, you get only one thing – an increased tendency to think always in terms of the other person's point of view, and see things from his angle as well as your own – if you get only that one thing from this book, it may easily prove to be one of the milestones of your career."[56]

Empathy – the ability to identify with another's point of view and with his or her feelings – is at once an emotional and symbolic skill, for the prerequisite of empathy is that one must decipher the complex cues of others' behavior. To be a good communicator means to be able to interpret others' behavior and their emotions. To be a good communicator requires a fairly elaborate coordination of emotional as well as cognitive skills: one can successfully empathize only if one has mastered the complex web of cues and signals through which others simultaneously hide and reveal their selves. Numerous guide-books to success in the corporation read like manuals in semi-otics with chapter headings such as "Signs and Signals," "How to Identify Cues and Clues," or "The Meanings behind the Words."[57]

In fact, self-awareness is adjacent to the injunction to iden-tify with others and listen to them. For example, an Internet site providing communication skills instructs:

> Good communication skills require a high level of self-awareness. Understanding your personal style of communicating will go a long way toward helping you to create good and lasting impres-sions on others. By becoming more aware of how others perceive you, you can adapt more readily to their styles of communicating. This does not mean you have to be a chameleon, changing with every personality you meet. Instead, you can make another person more comfortable with you by selecting and emphasizing certain behaviors that fit within your personality and resonate with another. In doing this, you will prepare yourself to become an active listener.[58]

Listening, or the capacity to mirror one's intentions and mean-ings, is deemed crucial to the ability to prevent conflict and create chains of cooperation. This is because listening to another enables one to generate what philosopher Axel Honneth calls "recognition," or "the positive understanding [that people have] of themselves." Because "self-image . . . is dependent on the possibility of being continually backed up by others,"[59] recognition thus entails an acknowledgment and reinforcement of another's claims and positions, on both the cognitive and emotional levels.

"The technique of active listening" has several functions.[60] First, the listener permits the venting of emotion. The speaker feels heard; tension is released. The listener's body posture and gestures such as head-nodding confirm for the speaker the sense of being heard. His feelings are reflected back by the listener (e.g., "It really was important for you that . . ."). She restates or paraphrases what the speaker has said, again checking with him for accuracy. She then asks clarifying questions for further information. The telling–listening function is extremely important in conflict resolution. This is particularly true where a continuing relationship between the parties is necessary, whether it be divorcing parents or ethnic communities in Bosnia.[61]

"Communication" instills techniques and mechanisms of "social recognition" by creating norms and techniques to accept, validate, and recognize the feelings of others. And as the previous quote also suggests, techniques of sociability, such as instilling social recognition, are skills applicable in a variety of social realms, from the domestic to the international via the political spheres. Communication is thus a cultural repertoire supposed to foster cooperation, to prevent or to resolve conflict, and to back up one's sense of self and identity. That is, at the same time that social interactions in the workplace increasingly demanded that the self perform its authentic interiority (in the form of emotions and needs), the therapeutic persuasion puts in place a mechanism of social recognition, whereby the self thus exposed could be shielded. In this way, communication is a way to define a mode of sociability in which an always precarious sense of self must be preserved. Communication thus defines a new form of social competence in which emotional and linguistic self-management aim at establishing patterns of social recognition.

But things are more complicated because "communication" is a slippery sociological centaur: it is justified on strategic grounds, as it is supposed to enable one to achieve and secure one's goals. Yet, the success of one's strategic goal is preconditioned on the implementation of a dynamic of recognition. It is this emotional, linguistic, and ultimately social competence which is supposed to help one achieve success inside the corporation. In a way, it is as if psychologists had managed to reconcile the two presumed incompatible aspects of Adam

Smith's philosophy – *The Theory of Moral Sentiments* and *The Wealth of Nations* – for they claimed that in developing skills of empathy and listening, one would further one's self-interest and professional competence. Professional competence was defined in emotional terms, by the capacity to acknowledge and empathize with others. Such emotional capacity to forge social relationships has become synonymous with professional competence writ large.[62]

Thus the concept and practice of communication, initially presented as both a technique and an ideal definition of self, is now even applied to characterize the ideal corporation. For example, the giant corporation Hewlett Packard presents itself in this way: "HP is a firm where one can breathe a spirit of communication, a strong spirit of interrelations, where people communicate, where you go towards others. It is an affective relationship . . ."[63] And to further illustrate my claim that communication has come to define the model of corporate selfhood, we may quote the following:

> In a recent survey of recruiters from companies with more than 50,000 employees, communication skills were cited as the single more [sic] important decisive factor in choosing managers. The survey, conducted by the University of Pittsburgh's Katz Business School, points out that communication skills, including written and oral presentations, as well as an ability to work with others, are the main factor contributing to job success.[64]

The reasons why communication has become so central in the definition of competent corporate selfhood are many: with the changing normative structure entailed in the democratization of social relationships, procedural rules had to be set up to reconcile the increasingly hierarchical structure of corporate organizations with the increasing democratization of social relations; moreover, given that professional competence and performance increasingly became constructed as outcomes and reflections of one's deep and true self, "recognition" became of paramount importance, since not only skills but "whole persons" were involved and evaluated in the work process. Finally, the increasing complexity of the economic environment, the ever-growing pace of new technologies and the consequent rapid obsolescence of skills made criteria for success changing and contradictory, and had the effect of overburdening the self with uncertainties, and of making it solely responsible for managing the uncertainties and tensions of the contemporary workplace. Communication has thus become an emotional skill with which to navigate in an environment fraught with uncertainties and conflicting imperatives and with which one can engage in collaboration with others through skills in instilling coordination and recognition.[65]

The economic sphere, far from being devoid of emotions, has been on the contrary saturated with affect, a kind of affect committed to and commanded by the imperative of cooperation and a mode of settling conflicts based on "recognition." Because capitalism demands and creates networks of interdependence,[66] and has affect within the very heart of its transactions, it has also brought about a destructuring of the very gender identities it helped establish in the first place. By commanding that we exert our mental and emotional skills to identify with others' point of view, the "communicative ethos" orients the manager's self to the model of traditional female selfhood. [More exactly, the ethos of communication *blurs gender divisions* by inviting men and women to control their negative emotions, be friendly, view themselves through others' eyes, and empathize with others. To give one example: "in professional relationships men don't have to be identified always with 'hard' masculine qualities and women with 'soft' feminine ones. Men can and should be just as capable as women of sensitivity and compassion ... and of the arts of cooperation and persuasion, while women should be just as capable as men of self-assertion and leadership and of the arts of competition and direction."[67] Emotional capitalism realigned emotional cultures, making the economic self emotional and emotions more closely harnessed to instrumental action.

Of course, I am not saying that the injunctions and instructions of advice literature straightforwardly shaped corporate life or that they miraculously erased the harsh and often brutal reality of the corporate world and of male domination of women. What I am saying though is that new models of emotionality which were formulated by a panoply of psychologists and consultants in management and human relations subtly but surely altered modes and models of sociability inside the middle-class workplace and reshuffled the cognitive and practical emotional boundaries regulating gender differences. Thus, when viewed through the prism of emotions, the capitalist workplace turns out to be far less devoid of emotions than has been conventionally assumed.

Let me now follow up on this remark and ask whether the view of the private sphere also changes when looked at through the prism of emotions. In its conventional account, capitalism produced a sharp distinction between private and public spheres. The woman ruled the private sphere, which contained and even stood for such emotions as compassion, tenderness, and selfless generosity. To quote Nancy Cott's seminal study on the middle-class private sphere, women were thus "removed from the arena of pecuniary excitement and ambitious competition. . . . [I]f man was the fiercest warrior, 'toil-worn' by 'troubled scenes of life,' women would scatter roses among the thorns of his appointed track."[68] But when actually viewed through the prism of emotions, these roses, cultivated in the private gardens of the family, turn out to have become peculiarly thorny.

The roses and thorns of the modern family

The intervention of psychologists in marriage

It seems almost a truism to suggest that therapeutic language is the privileged language to discuss the family. Not only has the therapeutic language been from its inception a family narrative, that is, a narrative of self and identity which anchors the self in childhood and in one's primary family relationships, but also a language geared to transforming the family (especially perhaps the middle-class family).

Interestingly enough, the twentieth century witnessed the emergence of another narrative which, like the therapeutic narrative, claimed to make new sense of the role of family structure in shaping the self, namely the feminist narrative.

In both therapeutic and second-wave feminist discourses, the family provides the root metaphor for the understanding of the pathologies of the self and is also the primary site for the self-transformations called for by these two persuasions. In 1946 the National Mental Health Act was passed.[69] While the work of psychologists until then had been limited to the army, to the corporation, and to the care of intense mental disorders, with the 1946 Act, the mental health of ordinary citizens extended the scope of psychologists' jurisdiction and marked a considerable advance of their power as a professional group. In the same way that Elton Mayo had wanted to promote efficiency and social harmony in the corporation, the new self-appointed healers of the psyche claimed to promote a greater harmony inside the family. Ordinary middle-class people, struggling with the ordinary problem of having a good life, were increasingly drawn inside the purview of psychologists' expertise. And indeed, as Helen Herman has documented, community mental health provided new services – psychotherapeutic – to a clientele that was better educated and more middle class.[70] During the 1950s and 1960s, federal legislation in turn provided the infrastructure necessary to support a community-oriented psychology and psychiatry, which helped psychology expand the scope of its influence to the "normally" neurotic middle-class people.[71] In other words, the sharp reorientation of psychologists' professional interests and clientele to "normal people" not only expanded the market of therapeutic services but also marked a shift in the social identity of the groups that consumed its services. By the 1960s, psychology had become fully institutionalized and had become an intrinsic aspect of American popular culture.

The full institutionalization of psychology in American culture had a mirror image in the equally full institutionalization of feminism in the 1970s. Indeed, by the mid-1970s a wide network of feminist organizations was in place: "women's clinics, credit unions, rape crisis centers, bookstores, newspapers, book publishers, and athletic leagues"[72] existed. Feminism had become an institutionalized practice, whose strength only grew with the establishment of departments of women's studies in universities, which in turn commanded a large array of other institutional practices inside and outside the university.[73]

In trying to understand the relationship between psychology and feminism, most analysts have paid attention to their history of mutual hostility. Yet it is almost as easy to find points of convergence between them. As the century unfolded, feminism and psychology proved to be ultimate cultural allies because women came to be the chief consumers of therapeutic advice, thus making therapy increasingly share common schemas with feminism, that is, basic categories of thought directly derived from the experience of women. On the other hand, because second-wave feminism was so densely located in the family and in the realm of sexuality, and because it positioned its narrative of emancipation within these spheres, it had natural affinities with the therapeutic narrative. Inasmuch as schemas can be transferable and transposable from one domain of experience to another, or from one institutional sphere to another, feminism and psychology could borrow from each other: for example, both psychology and feminism solicited the very kind of reflexivity which had been an attribute of women's consciousness. As art historian John Berger suggests, the woman is both "the *surveyor* and the *surveyed*" which are "two constituent yet always distinct elements of her identity as a woman."[74] Both feminism and therapy demanded that women be both surveyors and surveyed. Moreover, the therapeutic discourse, like feminism, constantly encouraged women to synthesize two contradictory sets of values, namely care and nurture on the one hand, and autonomy and self-reliance on the other. Independence and nurture were in fact the two central themes of feminism and therapy, and when properly synthesized would constitute emotional health and political emancipation. Finally, and perhaps most importantly, both feminism and therapy shared the idea and the practice of converting private experience into public speech, both in the sense that it was a speech with and for an audience, and in the sense that it was a speech to be committed to the discussion of norms and values which had a general, rather than particular, character. An obvious example of this process of converting private speech into a public one is the consciousness-raising group which was so important to grass-roots second-wave feminism.

Examples of how deep the therapeutic narrative runs within the feminist movement abound: veteran feminist activist and editor of *Ms.* magazine Gloria Steinem argued, in her 1992 autobiography *Revolution From Within*, that psychological barriers equally affect upper-class and lower-class women and that low self-esteem is the main problem that plagues women.[75] Or to take a very recent and widely publicized example, in her autobiography, peace and feminist activist Jane Fonda uses both feminist and therapeutic jargon to free herself from the debilitating effects of her distant father – Henry Fonda who did not hug her enough – and from her subsequent unhappy choices of three uncaring husbands. Finding her authentic voice becomes an emotional and political act.[76]

The mutual influence of therapy and feminism was most visible in the elaboration of a cultural model of emotional and sexual intimacy, which had as its background the emergence of the field of sexual therapy, itself related to the widely publicized Kinsey reports and, subsequently, to the study of sexuality by Masters and Johnson.[77] The notion of intimacy combined attributes both of the psychological discourse and of feminism, for liberated sexuality became a twin statement of emotional health and political emancipation. The new cultural model of intimacy was visible, for example, in a new cinematic formula focusing on disintegrating relationships, at the end of which women usually found their "freedom" and sexuality. (Woody Allen has perfected this genre with such movies as *Annie Hall, Another Woman, Manhattan, Alice*, etc.)[78]

To clarify what the new model of intimacy consisted of, let me take as example Masters and Johnson's *The Pleasure Bond* which was published in 1974 and which recycled their earlier findings on men's and women's sexuality and gave them a broader appeal.[79] For Masters and Johnson, the first step toward intimacy is to become aware of one's feelings and thoughts. And:

> [O]nce you're aware of your thoughts and feelings, let your partner know them. If you're afraid, say so. Perhaps together you can

discover what you are afraid of and why, and perhaps your partner can help you find ways of overcoming your fears gradually. Then as you move along the way, you will be acting in accordance with your feelings, not in spite of them.[80]

There was an important difference between the nineteenth century and the modern conception of the "true self" as exemplified by Masters and Johnson's conception of intimacy: for Victorians, finding and expressing the true self did not pose a special problem – the true self was always there and it was only to be entrusted to a person worthy of one's self-revelations.[81] But, in the new psychological imagination, the true self became opaque to its very bearer and now posed special problems. It required that one overcome a number of emotions – fear, shame, or guilt – which were most often unknown to the person in question and which required a new skill in the use of language. But the ultimate rationale for expressing and "digging out" these emotions was that intimate relations ought to be fundamentally egalitarian. What made the experience of intimacy both a psychological and a political affair was the fact that it stipulated that partners ought to relate to each other in an egalitarian fashion. The idea of equality in intimacy was apparent in two ways. One was that men were now called upon to pay far more careful attention to their inner self and feelings in a way that made them similar to women. For example, the 1974 *Liberated Man* by Warren Farrell condemned the pernicious effects of a system based on traditional men's values. Using a thoroughly therapeutic language, Farrell argued that men had been forbidden to cry or to expose their emotions, to show "vulnerability, empathy, or doubt."[82] Farrell required men to cultivate introspection, to be in touch with their true selves and to express all aspects of their selfhood.

Another way in which the new standards of equality were influencing definitions of intimacy was to be found in new definitions of women's sexuality. Although neither Masters nor Johnson professed to be feminists, they approached sexuality by casting it in the language of liberation and equality that had been the hallmark of the feminist movement. For example, "What a great many men and women must learn is that they cannot achieve the pleasure they both want until they realize that the most effective sex is not something a man does to or for a woman but something a man and woman do together *as equals.*"[83]

Sexual pleasure was thus predicated on the achievement of fair and equal relations, suggesting that therapeutic intimacy mobilized the language of rights and equated good sex with the affirmation of each partner's rights. Ultimately, such an ideal of sexual pleasure blurred gender differences. "[Virginia Johnson:] It's popular, I know, to point out the differences between men and women, but I have to tell you that from the beginning of our work, what has impressed us most have been the similarities, not the differences, between the sexes."[84] Through the ideal of intimacy, women were increasingly claiming not only equality but also similarity to men.

The cultural model of intimacy contains key motives and symbols of the two major cultural persuasions which shaped women's selfhood in the twentieth century (namely, psychology and liberal feminism): equality, fairness, neutral procedures, emotional communication, sexuality, overcoming and expressing hidden emotions, and centrality of linguistic self-expression are all at the heart of the modern ideal of intimacy. If in the corporation the language of therapy had initiated a realignment of masculinity around feminine conceptions of self, inside the family it encouraged women to claim the status of (male) autonomous and self-controlled subjects. If in the corporation, psychologists made productivity an emotional affair, in the realm of intimacy they predicated pleasure and sexuality on the implementation of fair procedures and on the affirmation and preservation of women's basic rights. More exactly, through the idea of "emotional health" or "healthy relationships," psychologists forcefully aimed to free intimate relationships from the long shadow of power and asymmetry. In this way, intimacy – or healthy relationships in general – became haunted by the problem of "equitable exchange" and by the problem of reconciling spontaneous emotionality with instrumental assertions of the self.

So far, this analysis may seem to be congruent with that of Giddens and others who have discerned in intimacy the movement toward equality and emancipation.[85] But in many ways, Giddens's analysis only resonates with the psychological credo that celebrates equality in intimate relationships and has failed to interrogate the very transformation of intimacy it purports to describe. The Weberian tradition to which I subscribe in general teaches us that we should not take the achievement of freedom or equality as our ultimate yardstick to evaluate social transformations. Rather, we should precisely inquire about the ways in which the new norms of equality or freedom have transformed the "emotional texture" of intimate relationships. In fact, I now argue that the intertwining of therapy and feminism has produced a vast process of rationalization of intimate relations. Because feminism and psychotherapy instructed a wide number of psychological, physical, and emotional strategies to transform the self, their recoding of the psyche entailed a "rationalization" of women's conduct inside the private sphere.

I will explain what I mean in the shortest way, with two examples, very typical of the advice literature on intimacy from the 1980s onward. In an article published in *Redbook* magazine, discussing a book by Dr Bessell (a psychologist), the author offers a questionnaire developed by the aforementioned Dr Bessell in order "to evaluate how compatible people are and how romantic their marriage is. The Romantic Attraction Questionnaire, or RAQ, which he uses to predict how well a couple are suited. The RAQ is composed of 60 statements . . . The ideal RAQ score is between 220 and 300 points, indicating a high enough level of romantic attraction to sustain a relationship."[86]

The second example reads as follows:

But how can Sheila satisfy Frankie's desires if he won't tell her what they are? You and your partner must also be able to tell each other exactly how you want to be loved. The following exercise will help you do that.

1   On a sheet of paper, complete each of the following sentences in as many different ways you can. Make your responses specific, concrete and positive.

- List those things your partner is currently doing that make you feel cared about and loved. "I feel cared about and loved when you . . ."
- Think back to when you and your partner were first dating. What did "your partner say or do then that he doesn't say or do now?" "I feel cared about and loved when you . . ."
- Now think of all those things you've always wanted your partner to do but were afraid to ask for. "I would feel cared about and loved if you would . . ."

2 Review your responses and rank them by number in order of their importance to you.

3 Read your responses to your partner. Put an X next to those your partner feels he cannot do for you just now.

4 Listen as your partner reads this list to you and indicate which of your partner's needs you cannot meet just now.

5 Exchange lists. Select three desires from your partner's list that you can agree to satisfy over the next three days.

Keep a list of your partner's list and agree to satisfy three new desires each week. Work toward being able to give your partner some of the things you originally felt reluctant to provide. The more difficult the request, the better you will feel once you have met it. Many couples report in fact that the partner's desires they thought were the most difficult to satisfy eventually become the things they most like to do for each other.[87]

To take these exercises seriously, we need not assume or presume that they are adopted wholesale by the readers of self-help literature. If they are significant, however, it is because they point to an important cultural transformation of the conduct of the self in intimate relationships. In fact, they point to the process of rationalization of intimate relationships which, I argue, is the result of the rise of egalitarian norms inside marriage (the feminist persuasion being the main advocate of such norms) and of the role which the method and lexicon of psychology have played in making sense of intimacy.

Rationalization includes five components:[88] the calculated use of means; the use of more effective means; choosing on a rational basis (that is on the basis of knowledge and education); making general value principles guide one's life; and, finally, unifying the previous four components in a rational methodical lifestyle. But rationalization has an additional important meaning: it is the process of expansion of formal systems of knowledge, which in turn lead to an "intellectualization" of everyday life.

What is striking about the exercises evoked above is that they demand and imply a *value rationalization* of personality. *Wertrationalitat* is the process of clarifying one's values and beliefs, and the process of making our ends conform to pre-established values. What do I want? What are my preferences and personality? Am I adventurous or in need of security? Do I need someone to be a breadwinner or someone with whom I can discuss the politics of the day? If these questions haunt advice literature, it is because women were enjoined both by feminism and by therapy to clarify their values and preferences, build relationships that conform to and suit those values, all with the goal of asserting an autonomous and self-reliant self. And this process can take place only when women carefully take themselves as objects of scrutiny, control their emotions, assess choices, and choose their preferred course of action.

Moreover, Weber viewed rationalization as characterized by a deeper refinement of techniques of calculation. Indeed, as the examples above suggest, intimate life and emotions are made into measurable and calculable objects, to be captured in quantitative statements. To know that I score a ten in the statement "I become anxious when you seem interested by other women" will presumably lead to a different self-understanding and corrective strategy than if I had scored two. Psychological tests of this kind use a specifically modern cultural cognition which sociologists Wendy Espeland and Mitchell Stevens called "commensuration." As they define it, "[C]ommensuration involves using numbers to create relations between things. Commensuration transforms qualitative distinctions into quantitative distinctions, where difference is precisely expressed as magnitude according to some shared metric."[89] Under the aegis of psychology and feminism, intimate relationships have increasingly become things to be evaluated and quantified according to some metric (which, by the way, varies with the wide gamut of psychologists and psychological schools available).

Finally, what is glaring in these two examples is the intertwining of textuality with emotional experience. Quoting medieval scholar Brian Stock, we may say that textuality has become an important adjunct of emotional experience.[90] "Writing down" an emotion "locks" it in space in the sense that it creates a distance between the experience of the emotion(s) and the person's awareness of that emotion. If literacy is the inscription of spoken language in a medium that enables one to "see" language (rather than hear it) and to decontextualize it from the act of speaking, similarly these exercises invite women to reflect on and discuss emotions after they are disconnected from their original context of occurrence. The reflexive act of giving names to emotions in order to manage them gives them an ontology, that is, seems to fixate them in reality and in the deep self of their bearer, a fact, we may claim, which goes against the volatile, transient, and contextual nature of emotions.

Indeed, literacy decontextualizes speech and thought, and detaches rules that produce speech from the very act of speaking.[91] (The obvious paradigmatic example of this separation of speech from speaking is grammar.) When locked into literacy, emotions become objects to be observed and manipulated. Emotional literacy makes one extract oneself from the flow and unreflexive character of experience and transform emotional experience into emotional words and into a set of observable and manipulable entities. Writing about the effect of print on Western thought, Walter Ong suggests that the ideology of literacy has given rise to the idea of the "pure text," that is, the idea that texts have an ontology, that their meanings can be detached from that of their authors and contexts. Similarly, the locking of emotions into written language gives rise to the idea of "pure emotion," the idea that emotions are definite discrete entities and that they are somehow locked and trapped inside the self, and that they can be inscribed in texts and apprehended as fixed entities, to be detached from the self, observed, manipulated, and controlled.

The control of emotions, the clarification of one's values and goals, the use of the technique of calculation, and the decontextualization and objectification of emotions all entail *an intellectualization* of intimate bonds, for the sake of a broader moral project: to create equality and fair exchange by engaging in a relentless verbal communication about one's needs, emotions, and goals. As in the corporation, communication is here a model of and a model for, at once describing relations and prescribing them. Sexual incompatibility, anger, money disputes, unequal distribution of domestic chores, personality incompatibility, secret emotions, childhood events – all of these ought to be understood, verbalized, discussed, communicated, and thereby, according to the model of communication, resolved. As a *Redbook* article put it: "Communication is the lifeblood of any relationship, and any love relationship particularly requires communication if it is going to flourish."[92]

Communication workshops or guidebooks offer numerous "exercises" which aim at making explicit the hidden assumptions and expectations of married people, at becoming aware of their speech patterns, at understanding how those in turn cause misunderstandings and alienation, at teaching the art and science of listening and, perhaps, most importantly, at using patterns of speech which are neutral (in order to offset negative emotions). As becomes clear, these techniques to improve marital communication aim at making the language exchanged into a neutral one, both emotionally and linguistically.

In the face of the inevitably intractable differences of biographies and personalities, the therapeutic persuasion suggests that, inside a marriage, a neutral ground of objective meaning can be reached. This neutral ground is both emotional and linguistic. For example:

This technique [called by the author Vesuvius] helps you identify when your anger is approaching volcanic proportions, and to ritualize it so that the focus is on getting your anger out of your system. Your partner's role is simply to witness respectfully the expression of your anger as if it were an overwhelming natural

phenomenon in which he or she is not a participant . . . If you
want to let off steam, say something like, "I'm really about to
explode. Can you listen to me for two minutes?" Any length of
time your partner will agree to is okay, but two minutes can feel
like a surprisingly long time to both the giver and receiver. If
your partner says yes, all he or she does is listen with awe, as if
watching a volcano explode – and let you know when your time
is up.[93]

This technique instructs that we contain negative emotions
and make them into objects external to the self, to be watched
from the outside, so to speak. This injunction to manage feelings by using neutral procedures of expression and speech is
at the heart of the communication and therapeutic ethos. This
is illustrated in the following example.

A technique called "The Shared Meaning technique [a technique to improve intimate relationships] enables you to share
the meaning of what you heard and check out if what you
heard is what your partner meant. Often it is not."[94] If we have
been told since post-structuralism that meanings are unintended, undecidable, and loaded with emotional inflections, by
contrast, the therapeutic techniques of communication decree
that ambiguity is the archenemy of intimacy and dictate that
we purge everyday language of unclear and ambivalent statements and of its possible negative emotional inflections and
that we reduce communication to its denoted meaning only.
This in turn suggests a somewhat paradoxical observation: the
therapeutic persuasion offers a variety of techniques to enable
awareness of one's needs and emotions, but it also makes emotions into objects external to the subject, to be observed and
controlled. Thus, the language in which emotions are
exchanged is simultaneously neutral and highly subjectivist –
neutral because one is supposed to attend to the objective and
denotative content of a sentence, and to try to neutralize the
subjective misinterpretations and emotions that can lurk in
the process; and subjectivist because the justification for
making a request, or experiencing a need or an emotion, is
always ultimately based on one's own subjective needs and
feelings. In order for these feelings to be "validated" and recognized, they do not require any higher justification than the

fact that they are felt by the subject. To "recognize" another means precisely not to argue with or contest the ground for one's feelings.

To summarize briefly: chaos, I think, is only superficially an organizing principle of intimacy.[95] Rather, because feminism and therapy are two main cultural formations which claimed to emancipate middle-class women from the yoke of traditional family arrangements, they contributed to rationalizing intimate relationships, that is, to submitting them to neutral procedures of examination and argumentation, predicated on an intense work of self-examination and negotiation. Such rationalization of emotional bonds has given rise to an "emotional ontology," or the idea that emotions can be detached from the subject for control and clarification. Such emotional ontology has made intimate relationships commensurate, that is, susceptible to depersonalization, or likely to be emptied of their particularity and to be evaluated according to abstract criteria. This in turn suggests that relationships have been transformed into cognitive objects that can be compared with each other and are susceptible to cost–benefit analysis. "When we use commensuration to help us decide things, value is based on the trade-offs we make between different elements of the decision."[96] Indeed, the process of commensuration makes intimate relationships more likely to be fungibles, that is, objects which can be traded and exchanged.

Conclusion

There are, I think, a number of conclusions to be drawn from this broad and cursory framework. My first observation is that the cultural persuasions of therapy, economic productivity, and feminism intertwined and enmeshed with one another and provided the rationale, the methods, and the moral impetus to extract emotions from the realm of inner life and put them at the center of selfhood and sociability in the form of a cultural model that has become widely pervasive, namely the model of communication. Under the aegis of the psychological model of "communication," emotions have become objects to be thought of, expressed, talked about, argued over, negotiated and justified, both in the corporation and in the family. While some argue that television and radio have been responsible for the sentimentalization of the public sphere, I suggest rather that it is therapy – joined with the language of economic accountability and with feminism – which has made emotions into micro public spheres, that is, domains of action submitted to a public gaze, regulated by procedures of speech, and by values of equality and fairness.

My second observation is that throughout the twentieth century, there has been an increased emotional androgynization of men and women, due to the fact that capitalism tapped into and mobilized the emotional resources of service workers, and to the fact that concomitantly to their entry into the workforce, feminism called on women to become autonomous, self-reliant, and conscious of their rights inside the private sphere. Thus, if the sphere of production put affect at the center of models of sociability, intimate relationships increasingly put at their center a political and economic model of bargaining and exchange.

One possible interpretation of all that I have discussed so far is that, thanks to the combined effects of the emancipatory structure of psychological knowledge, of feminism, and of the democratization of the workplace, emotional life has been brought within the purview of a dynamic of "recognition," a dynamic, which, as Axel Honneth suggests, is always historically situated, that is, shaped by the state of and language of rights. In other words, one may suggest that the model of communication which has pervaded work and marriage relationships contains and performs the new demand that one be recognized by others and recognize others.[97] If, as Habermas puts it, "communicative action . . . depends on the use of language oriented to mutual understanding,"[98] it is easy to see why the containment of negative emotions, empathy, and self-assertiveness may be viewed as emotional prerequisites for recognition. But I am not so sure that this is the case and I want to share with you here my hesitation. The model of "communication" which pervades the work sphere and the sphere of intimate relationships is fraught with ambivalence for, if it contains a method of entering into a dialogue with others, it also contains a language of rights and of economic productivity which is not easily compatible with the realm of interpersonal emotional relations. Let me explain. Emotions are by their very nature situational and indexical; they point to the ways in which the self is positioned within a particular interaction, and in that respect, they are a sort of shorthand for the self to understand how and where it is positioned in a particular situation. Emotions orient action by using tacit and concrete cultural knowledge of a particular object and making us take short-cuts to evaluate this object and act toward it (this theme will be more fully developed in lecture 3). In contrast, value-rationality, cognitive, and instrumental rationality and the process of "commensuration," all required to perform fluently the model of communication, form a cognitive style which empties relationships of their particularity and transforms them into objects which, because they are evaluated through standards of fairness, equality, and need-satisfaction, become more likely to know the fate of commodities traded.[99]

The process I have described has created a new and sharp split between an intense subjective life on the one hand and an increasing objectivization of the means to express and exchange emotions on the other. The therapeutic communication instills a procedural quality to emotional life which makes emotions lose their indexicality, their capacity to orient us quickly and unself-reflectively in the web of our everyday relationships. Instilling a panoply of procedures to manage emotions and to substitute for them adequate and standard speech patterns implies that emotions are increasingly disembedded and disentangled from concrete and particular actions and relationships. The precondition to "communication" is, paradoxically, the *suspension of one's emotional entanglements in a social relationship*. To communicate means to disengage from my position in a concrete and particular relationship and to take the position of an abstract speaker, affirming my autonomy or understanding. Ultimately, communicating means to suspend or bracket the emotional glue that binds us to others. Yet, at the same time, these neutral and rational procedures of speech are accompanied by an intensely subjectivist way of legitimating one's sentiments. For the bearer of an emotion is recognized as the ultimate arbiter of their own feelings. "I feel that . . ." implies not only that one has the right to feel that way, but also that such right entitles one to be accepted and recognized simply by virtue of feeling a certain way. To say "I feel hurt" allows little discussion and in fact demands immediate recognition of that hurt. The model of communication thus pulls relations in opposite directions: it submits relationships to procedures of speech which aim at neutralizing the emotional dynamic as that of guilt, anger, resentment, shame, or frustration, etc.; yet it intensifies subjectivism and emotivism, making us regard our emotions as having a validity of their own by the very fact of being expressed. I am not sure this is conducive to recognition for, as Judith Butler puts it, "recognition begins with the insight that one is lost in the other, appropriated in and by an alterity that is and is not oneself . . ."[100]

Thus the contemporary ideal of communication which has penetrated and saturated so thoroughly our models of social relationships may well be what anthropologist Michael Silverstein calls "a language ideology." A language ideology is a set of "self-evident ideas and objectives a group holds concerning roles of language in the social experiences of members as they contribute to say the expression of the group."[101] The language ideology of modernity might reside thus in this special belief in the power of language to help understand and control our social and emotional environment. How this has in turn transformed our identity is what I examine in the next lecture.

2 Suffering, Emotional Fields, and Emotional Capital

Introduction

In 1859, in a widely popular book called *Self-Help*, Samuel Smiles offered a series of biographies of men who had risen from obscurity to fame and wealth (self-help was masculine and women had little or no room in narratives of success and self-reliance). The book, which was immensely popular, made a powerful case for Victorian notions of individual responsibility. With the characteristic optimism and moral voluntarism of nineteenth-century faith in progress, Smiles evoked the "spirit of self-help in the energetic action of individuals."[1] Their lives, he wrote, inspire high-minded thinking and are examples of resolute working, integrity, and "truly noble and manly character." The power of self-help, Smiles went on, is the power of each to accomplish for himself. Thus the ideal of self-help had resolutely democratic overtones as it enabled even the "humblest of men to work out for themselves an honorable competency and a solid reputation."[2]

Some 60 years later, in the aftermath of the trauma of the First World War, Freud addressed his fellow psychoanalysts and offered a grandiose yet pessimistic vision of the task to come for psychoanalysis:

> Compared with the vast amount of neurotic misery which there is in the world, and perhaps need not be, the quantity we can do away with is almost negligible. Besides this, the necessities of our existence limit our work to the well-to-do classes . . . we care

nothing for the wider social strata, who suffer extremely seriously from neuroses.

Despite his call on democratizing psychoanalysis, Freud was skeptical about the poor man's willingness to part with his neurosis, "... because the hard life that awaits them if they recover offers them no attraction, and illness gives them one more claim to social help."[3] Where Smiles believed that the simple or the poor man could rise above the ordinary trials of everyday life through sobriety, endurance, and energy, Freud offered the disquieting possibility that neither the psychoanalyst nor the poor man may remedy "that vast amount of neurotic misery" because, Freud explained, laborers' social conditions are such that recovery from neurosis will only accentuate their misery. Contrary to Smiles's self-help ethos, which stipulated that moral strength could improve one's social position and social destiny, Freud held the pessimistic psychic and sociological view that the very capacity to help oneself is conditioned by one's social class and that, like other aspects of psychic development, such capacity can be damaged and, if damaged, it cannot be restored through sheer will power. Freud offers here a subtle sociological and psychological claim: for recovery to take place, he says, it must be convertible into a social benefit, thus not only suggesting an affinity between psychic disease, recovery, and one's socioeconomic position but also hinting that psychic misery can be capitalized on.

Thus, at the end of the nineteenth century and at the beginning of the twentieth, Smiles and Freud stood at opposite positions of the moral discourse of selfhood: Smiles's ethos of self-help made the access to mobility and to the market dependent on the exercise of virtue obtained by the combined effect of volition and moral spine. By contrast, self-help and virtue had no place in Freud's overall theoretical framework. This is because the family narrative that was at the heart of the Freudian outlook was not linear, but rather figurative, to use Erich Auerbach's word. Figurative is opposed to horizontal in that it "combines two events causally and chronologically remote from each other, by attributing to them a meaning common to both."[4] Whereas self-help postulated that life was a series of accumulated achievements and could be understood as incrementally unfolding along a horizontal time line, the Freudian view of self postulated that one had to draw many invisible vertical lines between key events in one's childhood and subsequent psychic development because one's life was not linear but cyclical. Moreover, for Freud, health, rather than success, was the new goal of the psyche and this health did not depend on one's sheer will, because healing occurs so to speak behind the back of the patient's cogito and will. Only transference, resistance, dream work, free association – and not "volition" and "self-control"– could lead to psychic and, ultimately social transformation. Finally, Freud tells us, psychic recovery cannot be democratic and evenly distributed throughout the social fabric. In fact, Freud suggests that therapy entertains a hidden affinity with social privilege.

Yet, if we take a snapshot of contemporary American culture, we may observe in it several ironic inversions of this state of affairs: in the self-help culture that has swept American society, Smiles's ethos of self-improvement and notions of Freudian inspiration have now become so intertwined as to be virtually indistinguishable. Moreover, precisely because of such alliance between the self-help ethos and psychology, psychic misery – in the form of a narrative in which the self has been injured – has now become a feature of the identity shared by both laborers and well-to-do people. Neglected childhood, overprotective parents, secret lack of self-esteem, compulsion to work, sex, food, anger, phobias and anxiety are "democratic" ills in that they no longer have clearly defined class membership. In this process of general democratization of psychic suffering, recovery has strangely become an enormously lucrative business and a flourishing industry.

How are we to explain the emergence of a narrative of identity which promotes, now more than ever, an ethos of self-help but which paradoxically enough is also a narrative of suffering? What is the articulation between emotional suffering and social class? How can we think of the connection between emotional life, class inequalities, and class reproduction? These are hopelessly broad questions and in the framework of one lecture I cannot hope to provide fully-fledged answers; here, I will simply try to delineate some general lines of thought to address these broad questions.

The self-realization narrative

In the American context, therapy could become a narrative of selfhood when it recycled and incorporated one of the major – if not the major – narrative of identity, namely the narrative of self-help. Therapy could become another version of the older self-help narrative when a number of factors intervened. First, there were internal changes in psychological theory which increasingly departed from Freudian determinism, and provided a more optimistic and open-ended view of self-development. Heinz Hartmann, Ernst Kris, Rudolph Loewenstein, Alfred Adler, Erich Fromm, Karen Horney, and Albert Ellis, although differing in outlook, all rejected the Freudian determinism of the psyche and similarly preferred a more flexible and open-ended view of the self, thus opening up new possibilities for a greater compatibility between psychology and the (distinctly American) moral view that people could and should shape their destinies. In particular it resonated with the mind cure movement which had been so popular during the nineteenth century and which stipulated that the mind could heal disease.

Such new psychological narratives which admitted the possibility for the self to change and shape itself could become diffused thanks to the "paperback revolution" which was initiated by Pocket Books in 1939 and which put easily affordable books within the reach of consumers. Using this paperback revolution, popular psychology could address and reach an ever-widening number of middle- and lower-middle-class people. Indeed, such books could be found everywhere, in convenience stores, railway stations, and drugstores, thus consolidating an already flourishing self-help industry.

The authority of psychologists became all the more pervasive so that by the late 1960s the political ideologies, which would have been likely to oppose individualist and psychological conceptions of the self, were on the wane. As sociologist Steve Brint put it, "Professional powers are most extensive . . . when professional experts are operating in a depoliticized environment of unchallenged premises . . . professional influence can be extensive when professionals are able to assert a central cultural value in the absence of a strong counterideology."[5] More exactly, if the 1960s had a political message, sexuality, self-development, and private life occupied a central place in it. The maturation and expansion of the consumer market, allied with the 1960s' "sexual revolution", contributed to increasing the visibility and authority of psychologists because these two cultural and ideological persuasions – consumerism and sexual liberation – had in common the fact that they made the self, sexuality, and private life into crucial sites for the formation and expression of identity. In this context, it was not only easy but also natural for psychologists to be drawn inside the new political discourse which chiefly addressed sexuality and the relation between the sexes. The claim to a free sexuality and self-realization would become closely associated with discourses which expanded the domain of the application of rights and extended the groups which were entitled to them. The movement which would help psychology make the deepest inroads in popular culture and which dramatically changed conceptions of the self was the Humanist movement, most noticeably in the persons of Abraham Maslow and Carl Rogers.

Carl Rogers viewed people as basically good or healthy and mental health as the normal condition of life, with mental illness, criminality, and other human problems as distortions of that natural innate tendency toward health. Moreover, his entire theory was built on a very simple idea of the self-actualizing tendency, which can be defined as the built-in motivation present in every life-form to develop its potential to the fullest extent possible. In a lecture given at Oberlin College in 1954, Carl Rogers suggested that:

> Whether one calls it a growth tendency, a drive toward self-actualization, or a forward-moving directional tendency, it is the mainspring of life, and is, in the last analysis, the tendency upon

which all psychotherapy depends. It is the urge which is evident in all organic and human life – to expand, extend, become autonomous, develop, mature – the tendency to express and activate all the capacities of the self . . . [this tendency] awaits only the proper conditions to be released and expressed."[6]

For Rogers, growth is a universal tendency, which is never really absent, only buried. The basis for maintaining such drive for growth was according to Rogers "to have a basic unconditional positive regard for oneself. Any 'conditions of worth' – I am worthy if I please my father, or I am worthy if I get a good grade – pose a limit to self-actualization," thus suggesting that the self was enjoined to strive now for an inexorable self-actualization.

But it was Abraham Maslow who would diffuse these and other similar ideas most successfully in American culture. Maslow's idea that there is a need for self-actualization led him to offer the hypothesis which would have a resounding success in US culture, namely that fear of success is that which prevents a person from aspiring to greatness and self-fulfillment. The result was to define a new category of people: those who did not conform to these psychological ideals of self-fulfillment were now sick. "The people we call 'sick' are the people who are not themselves, the people who have built up all sorts of neurotic defenses against being human."[7] Or as he also put it: "the concept of creativeness and the concept of the healthy, self-actualizing, fully human person seem to be coming closer and closer together, and may perhaps turn out to be the same thing."[8]

Such views of human development were able to penetrate and transform cultural conceptions of the self because they resonated with the liberal view that self-development was a right. This, in turn, represented an extraordinarily enlarged realm of action for psychologists: not only did psychologists move from severe psychological disorder to the much wider realm of neurotic misery. They now moved to the idea that health and self-realization were one and the same. People who had un-self-realized lives were now in need of care and therapy. To be sure, the idea of self-realization echoed the 1960s' political critique of capitalism and the demand for new forms of self-expression and well-being defined in non-material terms. But the therapeutic persuasion went further in that it cast the question of well-being in medical metaphors and pathologized ordinary lives.

In the injunction that we become our most "complete" or "self-realized" selves, no guideline was provided to help determine what differentiated a complete from an incomplete self. A new emotional hierarchy was drawn by psychologists – between self-realized individuals and those who struggled with a panoply of problems. But, and this is undoubtedly one of the most striking features of therapeutic culture, at the same time that it put health and self-realization at the center of a narrative of self, it also made a wide variety of behaviors into signs and symptoms of a "neurotic," "unhealthy," "self-defeating" self. In fact, when one examines the set of assumptions underlying most of the books using therapeutic language, a clear pattern structuring the therapeutic form of thought emerges: the ideal of health or self-realization defines *a contrario* a wide variety of dysfunctions. In other words, emotionally unhealthy behaviors are deduced from an implicit reference to and comparison with the model and ideal of the "fully self-realized life." If we transposed this ideal to the realm of physical health, this would be analogous to saying that someone who does not use the full potential of his muscles is sick,[9] with the difference that in the psychological discourse, the definition of what qualifies as a "strong muscle" is unclear and perpetually moving.

Let me provide a concrete example of such narrative. As I argued in the previous lecture, intimacy was posited by psychologists as an ideal to reach in sexual and marital relationships. In the context of close relationships, intimacy, like self-realization and other categories invented by psychologists, became a code word for "health." Healthy relationships were intimate and intimacy was healthy. Once the notion of intimacy was posited as the norm and the standard for healthy relationships, the absence of intimacy could become the organizing overall frame of a new therapeutic narrative of selfhood. In this narrative, an absence of intimacy now pointed to one's faulty emotional make-up, for example, to a *fear* of intimacy. Quoting a therapist, a *Redbook* article put the point aptly: "in our society, people are more afraid of intimacy than sex. . . . Typically, people with intimacy problems have trouble feeling sexual in close relationships, although they may function very well in more casual affairs."[10] Therapeutic narratives are tautological, for, once an emotional state is defined as healthy and desirable, all behaviors or states which fall short of this ideal point not only to unconscious emotions preventing one from reaching health, but also to a secret desire to run away from it. For example, a segment on Oprah Winfrey (aired on April 29, 2005) showed a slightly overweight woman with marital difficulties (the man did not like the fact that his wife had gained weight since their marriage). Given the implicit premise that intimacy is healthy and given that her weight was viewed as a barrier to intimacy, the woman's inability to lose her weight could in turn be the starting point for a narrative of psychological health: indeed, a psychologist invited on the show with the explicit purpose of framing her story as a psychological problem suggested that she harbored her weight as an unconscious retaliation against her husband. The "overweight" woman disagreed but only superficially: she concurred that there were unconscious reasons for her weight, but, she said, this was a way to push away potential suitors and to remain faithful to her husband. As in religious narratives, everything in the therapeutic narrative has a hidden meaning and purpose. In the same way that human miseries are explained by the assumption of a hidden divine plan, in the therapeutic narrative the choices that seem detrimental to us serve some hidden need and purpose. It is here that narratives of self-help and suffering connect for, if we secretly desire our misery, then the self can be made directly responsible for alleviating it. A woman who persistently falls in love with elusive or unloving men has thus only herself, if not to blame, at least to transform. The narrative of self-help is thus not only closely intertwined with a narrative of psychic failure and misery, but is actually put into motion by it. The contemporary Freudian legacy is, and ironically so, that we are the full masters in our own house, even when, or perhaps especially when, it is on fire.

Many have suggested that institutions build cultural coherence not so much by trying to establish uniformity as by trying to organize difference. Institutions are, in the words of Bill Sewell, "constantly engaged in efforts not only to normalize or homogenize but also to hierarchize, encapsulate, exclude, criminalize, hegemonize, or marginalize practices and populations that diverge from the sanctioned ideal."[11] What is interesting and perhaps unprecedented in the therapeutic persuasion is the fact that it has institutionalized the self through the generalized "difference" played against the background of a moral and scientific ideal of normality. By positing an undefined and endlessly expanding ideal of health, any and all behaviors could be labeled, *a contrario*, "pathological," "sick," "neurotic," or, more simply, "unadapted," "dysfunctional," or, more generally, "un-self-realized." The therapeutic narrative posits normality and self-realization as the goal of the narrative of self yet, because that goal is never given a clear positive content, it in fact produces a wide variety of un-self-realized and therefore sick people. Self-realization becomes a cultural category which produces a Sisyphean play of Derridean differences.

If they only live in the minds, cultural ideas are weak. They need to crystallize around objects, interaction rituals, and institutions. Culture, in other words, is embodied in social practices, and must work both practically and theoretically. The work of culture precisely lies in the ways in which it links these levels. Thus, culture extends from elaborate systems of thought to mundane acts of everyday life.[12] It is only within the context of a practical framework that a theoretical discourse becomes integrated in ordinary conceptions of the self.

The therapeutic narrative of self-realization is widely pervasive because it is performed in a wide variety of social sites such as support groups, talk shows, counseling, rehabilitation programs, for-profit workshops, therapy sessions, the Internet: all are sites for the performance and retooling of the self. These sites have become invisible yet pervasive appendices to the ongoing work of having and performing a self. Some of these sites take the form of self-organization in civil society (such as Alcoholics Anonymous), while others are now commodified social forms. To give one of the most successful and international examples of the latter: the Landmark Education Corp. (LEC) (also known as the Forum, formerly known as EST) offers a three-day workshop aiming at empowering people and grosses some $50 million a year in business. LEC is headquartered in San Francisco, and has 42 offices in 11 countries, thus suggesting that self-realization and its commodification have become a global enterprise. The Landmark Corporation, which offers a series of workshops for hefty sums of money, defines its purpose as being able to provide its participants with "a remarkable enhancement in their ability to communicate and relate to others, and to accomplish what's important to them in their own lives."[13] For the purpose of this research, I participated at one of these workshops. During the three days, the narrative of self-realization was put into motion by asking participants to focus on a dysfunctional aspect of their life (examples of how such narrative was produced included "I am single and cannot find a partner," "I have had many girlfriends but I cannot commit to any of them," "I have not talked to my father in five years because he does not approve of the way I live," "I am unhappy with my work and I'm unable to do anything about it") by having participants create a system of analogies between different, presumably recurring, aspects of their lives; and by having them adopt a narrative of self-realization to reshape their lives. For example, Daniel, who participated at the Landmark Corporation workshop, tells the following story on the web:

> One of my automatic ways of being came out of an incident when I was eleven, and I was forced to admit publicly to my friends that I was too shy to kiss a girl who lived across the street. I felt humiliated, and I concluded that I could never make it socially or really be brave with girls. So instead I re-designed myself to be studious, serious, hard-working and responsible as a way of compensating for this. Part of this was that I had to do things on my own, by myself. It became my winning formula. It still is, but since I can now distinguish it and see it, it doesn't have to run me anymore. I have the freedom to be in ways and create things which the previous automatic way of being would have forbidden

as off-limits or too threatening. I see myself as less rigid, and more able to enjoy integrating an increasing variety of people and activities in my social circle, my community, and my work.

We see in this story the therapeutic narrative at work: the narrative frame requires that a person identify a pathology, here an "automatic" way of being (automatic being constructed as opposite to self-determined). Once the automatic behavior is identified, the person builds causal connections with the past. He thus identifies a childhood incident in which the self was presumably diminished. That incident is in turn supposed to have had momentous consequences for the conduct of his life. This story is a good illustration of the ways in which any sorts of behavior, in fact even pro-social ones such as hard work, seriousness, and studiousness, are reframed as "pathological." Given that, normatively, hard work is commendable, it is here reinterpreted as "compulsive" for it to "qualify" as pathology. In conformity with the narrative structure provided by the Forum, this man also tries to identify the benefits accrued by his "pathological" behavior, thereby explaining why the behavior did not "feel" bad to him, and making himself responsible for changing it and for putting into motion the narrative of self-change and self-help.

In becoming diffused through the market, the therapeutic ethos moved from being a knowledge system to becoming what Raymond Williams has dubbed a "structure of feeling." The notion of structure of feeling designates two opposite phenomena: "feeling" points to a kind of experience that is inchoate, that is, that defines who we are without us being able to articulate this "who we are." Yet, the notion of "structure" also suggests that this level of experience has an underlying structure, that is, is systematic rather than haphazard.[14] Indeed, therapeutic self-help culture is an informal and almost inchoate aspect of our social experience, yet it is also a deeply internalized cultural schema organizing perception of self and others, autobiography, and interpersonal interaction.

In this vein, the therapeutic narrative structures the mode of speech and confession in a genre which has emerged in the last 15 years and has transformed the entire medium of TV, namely (maybe – and most evidently) television talk shows. The most successful and well-known example of this television genre is the Oprah Winfrey talk show which is viewed by more than 33 million people daily. Oprah Winfrey has notoriously used a therapeutic style of interviewing and has intensely promoted a therapeutic style of self-improvement.[15] Here is an example of the ways in which, like the Forum, the Oprah Winfrey show provides its guests with a therapeutic narrative to frame their self-understanding of their action. Sue wants to file for divorce. Her husband, Gary, feels distressed by the prospect and very much wants to go back to his wife. His desire to go back to his estranged wife is framed as a psychological problem, here under the broad heading of "why people want to get back to their ex." A psychotherapist, Ms Carolyn Bushong, has the primary function of framing Gary's story as a problem and of providing the general narrative accounting for his behavior:

> *Winfrey*: We've been joined by Carolyn Bushong. She's a psychotherapist, and her book is called *Loving Him without Losing You*. And she says that love is not usually the reason that people can't get over their exes. Is it?
>
> *Ms Carolyn Bushong*: Well, there are a lot of reasons, but a lot of it is rejection. And I think that's what's hooking him [Gary] in here – is that he need – you need to win her back to feel like you're OK with yourself . . . [later in the show] Gary is addicted to that. And "that" is that feeling that I'm a bad person. That – my ex says I'm a bad person. And maybe I am a bad person. So if I can convince her that I'm not a bad person, then they'll be OK again . . . in righting the wrong, it is the part, again, where maybe I feel guilty about what I did and I want to f – I want to make it up to that person so that my guilt can go away.
>
> *Winfrey*: Do you feel some guilt, too, Gary?
>
> *Gary*: Sure, I do.
>
> *Ms Bushong*: Yeah, about [you trying to control Sue].
>
> *Winfrey*: And you want to say, if you would just take me back, I can show you I won't do that anymore.
>
> *Gary*: That's the way I felt in the past, yes.
>
> *Winfrey*: Yeah, OK that you can't live or with – live with or without the ex.

Ms Bushong: And that gets into addicted – addictive relationships. There are so many relationships where people feel like, you know, "I want this person, I love them, but I hate them."[16]

A few elements are worth noticing here: therapeutic narratives create market niches, viewers who are simultaneously defined as potential patients and consumers. A group of people who "love too much" or people "who can't live without their ex" are simultaneously constituted as consumers and sick people by the profession of therapy, the publishing industry, and the television talk show. Moreover, we can also observe how the therapeutic narrative makes emotions, here guilt, into public objects to be exposed, discussed, and argued over. The subject participates in the public sphere through the construction and the exposure of "private" emotions. Finally, what helps one rewrite the story of his or her life as a therapeutic narrative is the goal of the story.[17] That is, it is such narrative goals as "sexual liberation," "self-realization," "intimacy," or "divorcing in an amicable way" which dictate the complication – what, in my life, prevents me from attaining the goal – which in turn dictates which past events of one's life one will pay attention to, and the emotional logic which will bind these events together ("I cannot get intimacy, because I am in fact afraid of intimacy; this is because my mother never attended to my needs when I was a child and because I was always craving her attention" or, "I should want to divorce in an amicable way; if I cannot do that, it is because I must have a problem, which is the real reason why I do not want this divorce"). In that sense, the therapeutic narrative is written backwards. This is also why therapeutic culture paradoxically privileges suffering and trauma. The very therapeutic narrative of self-realization can function only by identifying the complication in the story – what prevents me from being happy, intimate, successful – and make sense of it in reference to an event in one's past. It structurally makes one understand one's life as a generalized dysfunction, in order precisely to overcome it. This narrative foregrounds negative emotions as shame, guilt, fear, inadequacy, yet does not activate moral schemes or blame.

The therapeutic narrative is particularly suited to the genre of autobiography and has significantly transformed it. Indeed, in the therapeutic autobiography, identity is found and expressed in the experience of suffering and in the understanding of emotions gained by the telling of the story. If nineteenth-century autobiographical narratives were often interesting because they contained a "rags to riches" storyline, contemporary autobiographies take an opposite character: they are about psychic agony, even in the midst of fame and wealth. Three examples will clarify what I mean here: the first concerns Oprah Winfrey who, at the apex of her glory, could construct her life as follows:

> Before the Book [an autobiographical book she was supposed to write], she was emotionally adrift in the murky and suffocating waters of self-doubt. . . . What matters is how she felt inside, in the deepest corridors of her soul. And there, she never felt good enough. Everything flows from that: her perpetual struggle with obesity ("The pounds represented the weight of my life"), her sexually active adolescence ("It wasn't because I liked running around having sex. It was because once I started I didn't want the other boys to be mad at me"), her willingness to make a fool of herself for a man in the name of love ("I was in relationship after relationship where I was mistreated because I felt that was what I deserved"). "I know it appears I have everything," Oprah says, glancing around her $20 million, 88,000 square foot film and TV complex just west of downtown Chicago. "And people think because you're on TV you have the world by a string. But I have struggled with *my* own self-value for many, many years. And I am just now coming to terms with it."[18]

The narrative of psychic suffering recasts success biographies as biographies in which the self itself is never quite "made," and in which one's suffering becomes constitutive of one's identity. In the new therapeutic autobiography, success is not what drives the story; rather, it is precisely the possibility that the self can be undone in the midst of worldly success. For example, an actress as young and successful as Brooke Shields can write an autobiography when it contains an account of her postpartum depression.[19] In a similar way, Jane Fonda's biography[20] is told as the unfolding of an emotional drama which starts with an unhappy childhood spent with a cold and distant father, and which develops into three equally failed marriages. This is how Fonda's autobiography is sarcastically reviewed by the *New York Times* book reviewer:

> Fonda offers six decades' worth of exhaustive excavations into her lost and found selves. *My Life So Far* is not a lyrical title, but it captures Jungian Jane's Sisyphean, Oprah-phean struggle to process her pain and banish her demons. Her book is a psychobabble loop of . . . forfeiting her authenticity and feeling disembodied, then trying to reinhabit her body and "own" her womanhood and her space and her vagina, and her leadership and her wrinkles and her mother, so that her "authentic self" can emerge.[21]

All three biographies of powerful, successful, and glamorous women are thus told as tales of perpetual quest for the inner self, a struggle with one's emotional life, and the final psychic liberation from its emotional shackles. As Michel Foucault laconically remarked in his *History of Sexuality,* the care of the self, cast in medical metaphors of health, paradoxically encouraged a view of a "sick" self in need of correction and transformation.[22]

The narrative of self-help and self-realization is intrinsically a narrative of memory and of the memory of suffering. That is, at the epicenter of this narrative lies the injunction that one exercises one's memory of suffering in order to free oneself of it. To further illustrate the cultural distinctiveness of such narrative, one may quote here Abraham Lincoln's remark about his own life: "it is a great piece of folly to attempt to make anything out of my early life. It can all be condensed into a single sentence. . . . The short and simple annals of the poor."[23] The therapeutic narrative is radically opposed to this way of telling one's biography as it consists precisely in "making" everything "out of early life." Moreover, where Lincoln refused to adorn poverty with meaning, the therapeutic narrative consists precisely in making sense of ordinary lives as the expression of (hidden or overt) suffering. Given that the therapeutic narrative seems to be radically opposed to the ethos of self-sacrifice and renunciation which had dominated American culture until recently, how then can we explain its prevalence?

The therapeutic narrative has had a wide cultural resonance for a number of reasons:

1 It addresses and explains contradictory emotions – loving too much or not loving enough; being too aggressive or not being assertive enough. In marketing terms, it would be as if a cigarette was invented to satisfy both smokers and non-smokers, and as if smokers of different brands of cigarettes smoked the same cigarette.

2 These narratives use the cultural templates of religious narrative, a template that is both regressive and progressive: regressive because it is about past events which are, so to speak, still present and at work in people's lives; and progressive because the goal of the narrative is to establish prospective redemption, here, emotional health. In that way, these narratives are very efficient tools for establishing coherence and continuity for the self and for building a narrative that can encompass various stages of life cycles.

3 The narrative makes one responsible for one's psychic well-being, yet does that by removing any notion of moral fault. Thus, it enables one to mobilize the cultural schemes and values of moral individualism, of change and self-improvement. Yet, by transposing these to childhood and to deficient families, one is exonerated from the weight of being at fault for living an unsatisfactory life. This in turn enables the constitution of what we may call with David Held "communities of fate," or communities of suffering, best exemplified by the phenomenon of the support group.

4 The narrative is performative, and in that sense it is more than a story: it reorganizes experience as it tells it. In the same way that performative verbs do the very action they proffer, support groups provide a performative symbolic structure which performs the very healing which is the end and the goal of the narrative. It is in the experience of self-change and in the construction of that experience that

modern subjects experience themselves as being most morally and socially competent.

5   The therapeutic discourse is a contagious cultural structure because it can be duplicated and spread to collaterals, grandchildren, and spouses. For example, second- and third-generation Holocaust victims have now their own support group by virtue of the fact their grandparents were the actual victims of the Holocaust.[24] This is possible because they draw on a symbolic structure which enables them to constitute their identity as sick subjects to be healed. In this way, the therapeutic narrative can activate family lineage and continuity.

6   The therapeutic biography is almost an ideal commodity: it demands no or little economic investment – it demands only that the person allows us to peek into the dark corners of their psyche and that they be willing to tell a story. Narrating and being transformed by one's narration are the very commodities produced, processed, and circulated by a wide cohort of professionals (such as therapists, psychiatrists, doctors, and consultants) and by media outlets (women's and men's magazines, talk shows, radio call-in programs, etc.).

7   Finally, and perhaps most crucially, the therapeutic narrative emerges from the fact that the individual has become embedded in the culture saturated with the notion of rights. Both individuals and groups have increasingly made claims to "recognition," that is, demanded that one's suffering be acknowledged and remedied by institutions.

The therapeutic narrative is located at the tenuous, conflict-ridden and unstable junction between the market and the language of rights which saturates civil society. It is this narrative that is at the heart of what many have dubbed the cult of victimhood and the culture of complaint. For example, legal scholar Alan Dershowitz laments the fact that "it is virtually impossible to flip the TV channels during the daytime hours without seeing a bevy of sobbing women and men justifying their failed lives by reference to some past abuse, real or imagined."[25] In a similar vein, the art critic Robert Hughes suggests that our culture is an "increasingly confessional culture, one in which the *democracy of pain* reigns supreme. Everyone may not be rich and famous but everyone has suffered."[26] We can observe manifestations of this tendency even in philosophical thought. Žižek summarizes this by noticing that Richard Rorty defines a human being as "someone who can suffer pain and, since we are symbolic animals, as someone who can narrate this pain." And Žižek adds, given that we are potential victims, "the fundamental right becomes the right, as Homi Bhabha puts it, to narrate; the right to tell your story; to formulate the specific narrative of your suffering."[27]

The prevalence of suffering in popular or highbrow definitions of self-identity is undoubtedly hitting at one of the most paradoxical phenomena of the post-1980s era: namely, at the same time that the discourse of triumphant self-reliant individualism has never been so pervasive and hegemonic, the demand to express and perform one's suffering whether in support groups, talk shows, therapy, legal courts, and intimate relations has never been as strident. How then has this narrative become our primary way of expressing ourselves, of having a self, of having and expressing sentiments?

I suggest that the two claims to self-realization and to suffering must be viewed as institutionalized forms. For ideas to guide action, they require an institutional basis. My working assumption is that the self is a deeply institutionalized form.[28] For it to become a basic schema organizing the self, a narrative must have a great deal of cultural institutional resonance, that is, it has to become a part of the routine operations of institutions which command a great deal of cultural and social resources, such as the state or the market. Conversely, cognitive typifications such as a narrative of self should be viewed as institutions "deposited" in mental frames.[29]

The first and perhaps most pervasive institutional site responsible for the solidification of therapy in American culture was the state. The massive adoption of the therapeutic discourse by the state had to do with the fact that, in the postwar mood, there was great concern over the question of social adjustment and well-being,[30] which was made tangible by the creation of the National Institute of Mental Health in 1946. After the National Institute of Mental Health was created its funding grew at a spectacular rate. Whereas in 1950 the agency's budget was $8.7 million, in 1967 it was $315 million, thus suggesting that psychological health and services were deemed to be of universal value and application. This spectacular growth was connected with the fact that the state increasingly used therapy in many of the services it offered, such as social work, prison rehabilitation programs, education, and courts. In fact, as Michel Foucault and John Meyer have argued in different yet congruent styles, the modern state organized its power around cultural conceptions and moral views of the individual. The psychological discourse provided one of the main models for individualism, adopted and propagated by the state.[31] These models, as Meyer and his associates argue, are present in the agenda and in the mode of intervention of the state in various domains such as education, business, science, politics, and international affairs. But the state is not the only actor, although it is the strongest one, to have expanded the therapeutic way of constructing human problems. Actors in civil society have promoted the therapeutic narrative as well.

Feminism was one of the major political and cultural formations to adopt the therapeutic discourse, as early as the 1920s and most forcefully in the 1960s, in its promotion of sexuality as the site of emancipation (see previous lecture) and later in the 1980s when it denounced the oppressive effects of the patriarchal family in the abuse of children. Using the defense of abused children, feminism found in therapy a new tactic to criticize the family and patriarchy. This, I surmise, is because the category of "child abuse" enabled feminism to mobilize cultural categories — for instance, that of the child — which had a broader and more universal appeal.

One of the most forceful feminist advocates against child abuse was Alice Miller who, in her widely influential *The Drama of the Gifted Child*, declared, following the therapeutic logic, that when a child is abused, in order to survive and avoid the unbearable pain, the mind is provided with a remarkable mechanism, the "gift" of "repression", which stores these experiences in a place outside consciousness.[32] Miller put trauma at the center of the life narrative, and made repression the explanation of the fact that some abused or neglected children do not feel, as adults, victims of trauma. And as in the Humanist narrative, Miller viewed authenticity as the true goal toward which the self should aspire. Following therapeutic logic, she also saw psychic problems transmitted from one generation to the next: "Any person who abuses his children has himself been severely traumatized in his childhood in some form or another."[33] Feminists used the category of trauma to criticize the family, to protect the child, to pass new legislation, and to fight male violence against both women and children. In enlarging their political critique of the family and in their wholesale adoption of the category of "emotional damage," feminists inevitably increasingly drew on and relied on the language of psychology.

The third group which was instrumental in promoting the therapeutic narrative was the Vietnam veterans who used the category of trauma to receive social and cultural benefits. In 1980, the American Psychiatric Association officially recognized the category of trauma:

> The establishment of PTSD resulted, in part, from intense lobbying by mental health workers and lay activists on behalf of Vietnam War veterans. The PTSD diagnosis acknowledged and dignified the psychological suffering of American veterans amid their ambivalent reception by a divided and war-weary populace. It grounded their puzzling symptoms and behaviors in tangible external events, promising to free individual veterans of the stigma of mental illness and guaranteeing them (in theory, at least) sympathy, medical attention, and compensation.[34]

Following the institutional and epistemological logic of the therapeutic discourse, PTSD became progressively applied to a wide variety of occurrences, such as rape, terror attacks, accidents, crime, etc.

The final and perhaps most significant actors to enter the arena of mental suffering were the pharmaceutical industry and the DSM, which gave a remarkable market impetus to the field of mental health. The DSM was established in 1954 and is a diagnostic manual which grew out of the need to make the relationship between diagnosis and treatment tighter in order for insurance companies or other payers to process claims more efficiently. Not only is DSM now used by the majority of mental health clinicians but it is increasingly used by "state legislatures, regulatory agencies, courts, licensing boards, insurance companies, child welfare authorities, police, etc."[35] The codification of pathologies grew out of the fact that mental health became tightly connected with insurance coverage. DSM – which provides the code numbers to be listed on the claims for insurance reimbursement – is the bridge between mental health professionals and such large money-giving institutions as Medicaid, Social Security Disability Income, benefit programs for veterans, and Medicare.[36] As Kutchin and Kirk put it, "DSM is the psychotherapist's password for insurance reimbursement."[37]

I would argue that the main cultural impact of the various versions of DSM – especially of DSM III – was to expand considerably the range of behaviors defined as mental disorder. Thus, in DSM III, one could now find described as a mental disorder such behaviors as "oppositional disorder" (coded 313.81) defined "as a pattern of disobedient, negativistic, and provocative opposition to authority figures,"[38] or "histrionic personality disorder" (coded 301.50), where individuals affected by this disorder are "lively and dramatic and always drawing attention to themselves,"[39] or still "avoidant personality disorder" (coded 301.82) where the essential feature is "hypersensitivity to potential rejection, humiliation, or shame; an unwillingness to enter into relationships unless given unusually strong guarantees of uncritical acceptance."[40] These examples alone suggest how the DSM considerably enlarged the category of mental disorder. The making of the DSM coincided with the interests not only of a wide variety of clinical workers – psychiatrists, clinical psychologists, social workers – and insurance companies, who wanted to regulate more closely the realm of mental health, but also those of pharmaceutical industries, eager to tap into the market of emotional and mental disease. Pharmaceutical industries have a chief interest in the expansion of mental pathologies which can then be treated with psychiatric medications.[41] "[F]or drug companies . . . unlabeled masses are a vast untapped market, the virgin Alaskan oil fields of mental disorder."[42] The DSM thus contributed, willfully or not, to the labeling and charting of new mental and consumer territories which in turn helped expand the market of pharmaceutical companies.

I think that we have here an outstanding example of what Bruno Latour and Michel Callon call a "process of translation," namely the fact that individual or collective actors constantly work to translate their own language, problems, identities, or interests into those of others.[43] Feminists, psychologists, the state and its armies of social workers, academics working in the field of mental health, insurance companies and pharmaceutical companies "translated" the therapeutic narrative, because all, for different reasons, have a strong interest in promoting and expanding a narrative where the self is defined by pathology, thereby de facto promoting a narrative of disease. For, in order to be better – the main commodity promoted or sold in this new field – one must first be sick. Thus, at the very same time that these actors promoted health, self-help and self-realization, they also by necessity encouraged and expanded the realm of psychic problems. In other words, the narrative of therapeutic self-help is not, as structuralists would have it, the opposite of "disease" in a conceptual pair of opposites. Rather, the very same narrative that promotes self-help *is* a narrative of disease and psychic suffering. Because cultural schemata can be extended or transposed to new situations, feminists, veterans, courts, state services, professionals of mental care appropriated and translated the same schemata of disease and self-realization to organize the self, making the narrative of self-realization a truly Derridean entity, containing and enacting simultaneously that which it wants to exclude, namely disease, suffering, and pain.

I am skeptical about the thesis put forth by many, such as Philip Rieff, Robert Bellah, Christopher Lash, Philip Cushman, or Eli Zaretsky, to the effect that the therapeutic ethos deinstitutionalizes the self. On the contrary, rarely has a cultural form been so institutionalized. Moreover, contra Foucault, the therapeutic narrative produces, not pleasure, but a multiplicity of forms of suffering. Where Foucault argued that "we have . . . invented a different kind of pleasure: pleasure in the truth of pleasure, the pleasure of knowing the truth, of discovering and exposing it,"[44] I would argue that the therapeutic narrative has produced a multiplicity of forms of suffering, for we can say with anthropologist Richard Schweder that "[a] people's causal ontology for suffering plays a part in causing the suffering it explains, just as people's representations of a form of suffering may be part of the suffering it represents."[45] In other words, because psychology's principal vocation has been to alleviate a variety of forms of psychic suffering through an undefined ideal of health and self-realization, and because the therapeutic persuasion has in fact contributed to the creation of a personal memory of suffering, it ironically creates much of the suffering it is supposed to alleviate. I believe it is morally and epistemologically wrong to subsume such forms of suffering under pleasure, only because they are intertwined with a project of self-knowledge or self-help.

To summarize: We cannot separate the narratives of suffering from that of self-help and the threads connecting them are many and contradictory: the extension of human rights to new domains, such as children's rights and women's sexuality, the commodification of mental health by pharmaceutical companies, the regulation of the profession of psychologist by insurance agencies, the increasing intervention of the state as an educator in a wide variety of domains ranging from the private to the public, all of these constitute the hidden dynamics explaining how the narrative of victimhood has become so pervasive and why such narrative smoothly coexists with a narrative of self-help.

Emotional fields, emotional habitus

These various actors all converged in the creation of a realm of action in which mental and emotional health is the primary commodity circulated. They all contributed to the emergence of what I call an emotional field: that is, a sphere of social life in which the state, academia, different segments of cultural industries, groups of professionals accredited by the state and university and the large market of medications and popular culture intersected to create a domain of action and discourse with its own rules, objects, and boundaries. The rivalry between various schools of psychology, or even the rivalry between psychiatry and psychology, should not hide the fact that they ultimately agree on defining emotional life as in need of management and control and on regulating it under the incessantly expanding ideal of health. A great variety of social and institutional actors compete with one another to define self-realization, health, or pathology, thus making emotional health into a new commodity produced, circulated, and recycled in social and economic sites which take the form of a field. The narrative of suffering should be viewed as the outcome of the extraordinary convergence between the different actors positioned in the field of mental health.

Fields, Bourdieu tells us, maintain themselves through the mechanism of habitus or "the structuring mechanism that operates from within agents."[46] Not only do emotional fields work by constructing and expanding the realm of the pathological and by commodifying the realm of emotional health, but also by regulating access to new forms of social competence which I will dub emotional competence. In the same way that cultural fields are structured by cultural competence – the capacity to relate to cultural artifacts in a way that signals familiarity with high culture sanctioned by the upper classes – emotional fields are regulated by emotional competence, or the capacity to display an emotional style defined and promoted by psychologists.

Like cultural competence, emotional competence is translatable into a social benefit, as professional advancement or social capital. Indeed, for a particular form of cultural behavior to become a capital, it must be convertible into economic and social benefits; it must be convertible into something that agents can play with in a field, that will give them a right of entry, or will disqualify them, or will help them seize what is at stake in that field.[47] Even more than traditional forms of cultural capital – such as wine-tasting or familiarity with high culture – emotional capital seems to mobilize the least reflexive aspects of habitus. It exists in the form of "long-lasting dispositions of mind and body" and is the most "embodied" part of the embodied forms of cultural capital.[48]

In the American context, emotional competence is most formalized in the workplace, and most particularly in the personality tests that were instituted to hire people in corporations. Personality tests are to emotions what scholastic tests are to cultural capital, namely a way to sanction, legitimize, and authorize a specific emotional style, an emotional style which in turn has been shaped by the psychoanalytical persuasion. As Walsh and Betz, two experts in personality research, suggest, "psychoanalytic concepts and psychoanalysis itself have had a rather profound impact on the assessment process."[49] In other words, even if the spirit presiding over personality tests seems to be far away from that of psychoanalysis, it remains that psychoanalytical concepts played an important role in making personality and emotional assessments into tools to recruit and evaluate job performance. Emotional behavior has become so central to economic behavior that when the notion of emotional intelligence emerged in the 1990s, it overtook the American corporation. It was a journalist with a training in clinical psychology, Daniel Goleman, who, with his book entitled Emotional Intelligence, contributed to formalize what had been in the making throughout the twentieth century, namely the creation of formal instruments of classification of emotional behavior and the elaboration of the notion of emotional competence. If this book almost single-handedly turned the notion of emotional intelligence into a central concept of American culture overnight, it was because clinical psychology had already instilled and naturalized the idea that emotional competence was a crucial attribute of the mature self. Emotional intelligence "is a type of social intelligence that involves the ability to monitor one's own and others' emotions, to discriminate among them, and to use the information to guide one's thinking and actions."[50] Emotional intelligence involves abilities that may be categorized into five domains: self-awareness; managing emotions; motivating oneself; empathy; handling relationships. Through the notion of emotional intelligence, one could now measure properties of a social and cultural world that had been massively transformed by psychologists, thus creating new ways to classify people.

[Emotional intelligence is an instrument of classification[51] which, like the notion of IQ, is able to stratify social groups by the simple virtue of being translated in organizational roles, advancement, and responsibilities.]In the same way that IQ served to classify people in the army and in the workplace so as to increase their productivity, EI quickly became a way to classify productive and less productive workers, this time by emotional rather than cognitive skills. EI was converted into an instrument of classification inside the workplace and was used to control, predict, and boost performance. In this way, the notion of emotional intelligence brings the process of commensuration of emotions (discussed in lecture 1) to its ultimate end, making them categories to be ranked, classified, and quantified. For example, in a business article the author claims that "Experienced partners in a multinational consulting firm were assessed on the EI competencies plus three others. Partners who scored above the median on 9 or more of the 20 competencies delivered $1.2 million more profit from their accounts than did other partners – a 139 percent incremental gain."[52]

In the same way that the rise of credentials was accompanied by new forms and instruments of classification around the notion of intelligence (giving rise to the famous IQ which in turn serves as a way to classify and hierarchize different social positions), the emotional capitalism I have been describing gives rise to the notion of emotional intelligence and introduces new forms of classification and distinction. By making personality and emotions into new forms of social classification, psychologists not only contributed to making emotional style a social currency – a capital – but also articulated a new language of selfhood to seize that capital. For example:

At L'Oreal, sales agents selected on the basis of certain emotional competencies significantly outsold salespeople selected using the company's old selection procedure. On an annual basis, salespeople selected on the basis of emotional competence sold $91,370

more than other salespeople did, for a net revenue increase of
$2,558,360. Salespeople selected on the basis of emotional com-
petence also had 63 percent less turnover during the first year
than those selected in the typical way.[53]

This example is telling because it shows not only that emotional competence has indeed become a formal criterion for
recruiting and promoting people inside the workplace but also
that emotional forms of capital can be converted into monetary
ones.

Emotional intelligence is not only the kind of competence
required in an economy in which the performance of the self
is crucial to economic performance but also the outcome of
the process of intense professionalization of psychologists
who, historically, have been extraordinarily successful in
claiming the monopoly over the definition and the rules of
emotional life and who thus have established new criteria to
capture, manage, and quantify emotional life. To be emotionally intelligent has especially become the prerogative of a professional class responsible for the management of emotions
– especially of the new middle classes – and being emotionally
competent consists in displaying the cognitive and emotional
skills of which clinical psychologists are the virtuosos. Emotional intelligence reflects particularly well the emotional style
and dispositions of the new middle classes which are located
in intermediary positions, that is, which both control and are
controlled, whose professions demand a careful management
of the self, who are tightly dependent on collaborative work,
and who must use their self in both a creative and a productive
way. Emotional intelligence is then a form of habitus that
enables the acquisition of a form of capital situated at the seam
line between cultural and social capital. It is cultural because,
as Bourdieu has suggested (without theorizing it), modes and
codes of cultural evaluation have an emotional style or tonality
(as when Bourdieu refers to "detachment" or to "participatory
identification"). One's emotional attitudes and style, like one's
cultural taste, define one's social identity.[54] It is social, because
emotions are the very stuff of which social interactions are
made and transformed. If cultural capital is crucial as a status

signal, emotional style is crucial to how people acquire networks, both strong and weak, and build what sociologists call social capital, that is, the ways in which personal relationships are converted into forms of capital, such as career advancement or increased wealth.[55] Such capital has become particularly prominent in a form of capitalism which can be characterized, following Luc Boltanski's expression, as "connexionist." As he puts it, in connexionist capitalism, the class habitus of the dominant classes can no longer rely on its own intuition. This habitus needs to know how to establish relationships between people not only geographically but also socially distant from oneself.[56]

The pragmatics of psychology

It would be tempting to stop the analysis here, with the constructionist conclusion that the social world is made up of social struggles, and that what is at stake in social fields is, as Bourdieu has said repeatedly, arbitrary. But I think that stopping our analysis at the constructivist moment is unsatisfactory. Rather, we should ask, in the footsteps of pragmatism, why certain meanings "work." To be efficacious, a discourse must accomplish certain things for the people who believe in it and use it. A discourse will keep functioning and circulating if it "accomplishes" certain things that "work" in people's everyday life. Let me thus ask: What does the therapeutic emotional competence accomplish?

If we take intimate relationships – including lovers, spouses, or children – to be *a sphere of action and meaning in its own right*, as well as a cultural and social resource to help people achieve well-being, we may inquire about the cultural and symbolic forms that grant access to such spheres of well-being. Such a proposition runs counter to the conventional paradigm of the sociology of domination which usually addresses various forms of capital in the context of competitive arenas and is more uncomfortable approaching well-being or the family as forms of goods in their own right. For example, Bourdieu's theory of social reproduction approaches the family as an institution that is ultimately subordinate to social structure. In the theory of symbolic reproduction, the family is the institution that instills the early and invisible dispositions that will later be converted into practical choices in competitive fields of social struggle. However, as Michael Walzer[57] and such feminist theorists as Susan Okin have so persuasively suggested, a theory of justice ought to account for and respect the values of each sphere of life and distinguish between the goods at stake in the market and those at stake, say, in the family.

If we approach the family and intimacy as autonomous spheres of meaning and action, we may then analyze them as *moral goods* in which the content of *selfhood and well-being* are at stake. That is, if we reverse the Bourdieusian model and inquire about the ways in which certain professions socialize their children to a certain emotional habitus, which in turn will help them reach particular forms of *eudaimonia* (happiness, well-being) in the realm of intimate relationships, then we may inquire about the ways in which intimacy or friendship are, like other forms of goods, socially distributed and allocated.

Let me illustrate what I mean here with an interviewee, a woman, who is an editor and has a PhD in English Literature from a top mid-western university, and has been married for four years to a professor of philosophy.

Interviewer: Do you have negative emotions?
[*Silence*]
Int: You don't have to answer if you don't want to.
Respondent: Well, I am not sure if I should say.
Int: It is completely up to you.
Res: Well – I am jealous. I am very jealous. And I know where it comes from. It basically comes from my father leaving my mother for another woman, and growing up with a mother who told me over and over again not to trust men.
Int: Does it have any impact on your relationship with your husband?
Res: Yes, oh yes, I can become very jealous, very possessive, and feel really threatened by other women. Like the other day, we were having dinner with friends of ours, and one of my friends

asked Larry [her husband] if he had been to India. And he said he had but he did not want to talk about it, because he had been there with a girlfriend, and he knew it would upset me to talk about it. So he didn't want to talk about it, but she kept asking him questions, until I told her: "Look, he does not want to talk about it. He was there with a girlfriend, and that's making me upset." Larry and I, we had some rough times over this issue.

Int: Did you do something about it?

Res: Yeah – Just talking, we talked for a long, long time about it. Both of us are sort of very aware of ourselves; both of us have a strong interest in psychoanalysis and therapy; so we talked and talked about it, and analyzed it. So it was just talking about it, understanding it, and having him tell me over and over again that he loved me, and that he would not leave me for another woman. And I think that the fact we could talk about our feelings and really understand them is what got us through.

This highly educated couple displays what I have called "emotional competence" (dubbed in the psychological persuasion "intelligence"), namely self-awareness, the ability to identify their feelings, talk about them, empathize with each other's position and find solutions to a problem. The therapeutic language and this couple's emotional intelligence are "real" cultural resources, not because they understand the "real" nature of their emotional problems, but because they can deploy a common cultural structure to make sense of their difficult emotions and put them "to work" by eliciting a narrative of suffering and self-help, which they can in turn both share and capitalize on to further their intimacy.

In other words, emotional competence is not only a form of capital which can be converted into social capital or advancement in the work sphere, but also can be a resource to help ordinary middle-class people reach ordinary happiness in the private sphere. Compare this response with that of a working-class man, George a 50-year-old janitor:

Respondent: . . . and the second [wife] she left me – I didn't leave her. I mentioned that I left her but I didn't leave her. She left me. I came home one morning from work at two o'clock in the morning and she had took a lot of stuff that she shouldn't have took and didn't tell me anything about it. See, so I would've told her.

Interviewer: And she did not tell you anything beforehand that indicated that she might leave?

Res: No. No.

Int: So how do you explain her leaving?

Res: She left. And she didn't tell me anything about it. That's the only thing I can think. [*Later in the interview*] After she left – after I got the initial shock and it wasn't so much the shock about her going, it – it was the shock over what she done, you know. That's the thing that upset me more than anything else.

Int: What had she done?

Res: Well, uh – uh – you know, uh – I mean the way she didn't sit down and talk to me. She could've told me about. I would've felt much better if she would've told me – if she says, "George, uh – uh, I am not satisfied with situation and I'm going to move." I would've loved her to come straightforward and told me. Cause that's the way I – I told her on several occasions that I wasn't satisfied and, uh, you know –

Int: And how did she tell you?

Res: I don't know. I don't know.

Int: You don't know. And what is the thing that is difficult in having her move out without telling you?

Res: It makes me feel like I can trust very few women or for that percentage trust anybody because once you sleep with some-body every night and all of a sudden then you come home one day, that's a horrible feeling. It's like "I let you break into my house and then you devastate my sixty years on earth." It's like leaving like she did – I come home from work and somebody has broken the house and taken a lot of stuff out of it. It's something that I worked hard for, you know what I mean? That's a devastating feeling. You know. Those are the two – outside the bathroom when I picked up the wreaths at the hospital and they told me that my wife was deceased in an automobile accident – those were the biggest shocks in my entire life.

What is striking here is the fact that this man could not put up any explanatory framework to rationalize and come to terms with his pain at having been left. He could experience the departure of his wife as inexplicable shock, all the more powerful and painful because he could not wrap it into meaning. When juxtaposed, these two examples show that the therapeutic model of communication is not, as social constructionists would have it, a ploy to make us "disciplined," "narcissistic," or subject to the psychologists' interests. Rather, the therapeutic model is "good for" addressing the volatile nature of selfhood and of social relationships in late modernity. It is "good for" structuring divergent biographies, providing a technology to reconcile individuality with the institutions in which it operates, for coping with the disruptions that have become inherent in modern biographies, and, perhaps most importantly, for preserving the self's standing and sense of security, rendered fragile precisely by the fact that the self is continually performed, evaluated, and validated by others. As Richard Sennett put it, "The problem we confront is how to organize our life histories now, in a capitalism which disposes us to drift."[58]

If the therapeutic model is so pervasive, it is not – or at least not only – because it serves the interests of many different groups and institutions, but also because it mobilizes the cultural schemata of competent selfhood and helps order the chaotic structure of social relationships in late modernity. To debunk the way in which psychology is played in and by institutions should not make us, sociologists, oblivious to the role it plays in an economy of personal problems. If we do not want psychology to pull the rug from under our feet, we should ultimately try to reformulate a critique of social injustices by inquiring into the ways in which access to psychological knowledge may perhaps stratify different forms of selfhood.

Conclusion

Let me conclude somewhat paradoxically, with Freud, rather than with Marx. In his *Introductory Lectures*, Freud imagines a house divided between "basement" and "first floor"; the caretaker's daughter lives in the basement and the landlord's daughter on the first floor.[59] Freud imagines that, early in their lives, the two girls engage in sexual play. But, Freud tells us, they will develop quite differently: the caretaker's daughter who does not think much of playing with genitals will emerge unharmed – and Freud even goes as far as imagining that she may become a successful actress and eventually an aristocrat. By contrast, the landlord's daughter, who has learned early on ideals of feminine purity and abstinence, will view her childhood sexual activity as incompatible with such ideals, will be haunted by guilt, take refuge in neurosis, will not marry, and, given Freud's own and his contemporaries' prejudices, we are led to presume that she will live the lonely life of a spinster. Thus, Freud suggests that the social destiny of the two girls is intertwined with their psychic development, the neurosis or lack of it determining each woman's social trajectory. Freud suggests that members of different classes have access to different, if not unequal, emotional resources and that the lower classes are, so to speak, emotionally better equipped than the middle classes, for it is precisely their lack of sexual inhibition that will prevent the birth of neurosis and will in turn help the caretaker's daughter achieve upward social mobility.

Freud makes an interesting and complex claim about the relation between social and psychic trajectories. He points to *some* connections between emotions and social position: he suggests not only that class determines emotions, but also that emotions may play an invisible but powerful role in disturbing class hierarchies and in social mobility. By suggesting that middle-class morality of emotions – which was functional to the capitalist work sphere (because one has to learn renunciation and self-control) – is incompatible with successful personal and emotional development, Freud tells us that the middle- and upper-middle-class domination of the social and economic realms may ultimately be detrimental not only to fulfillment and happiness but ultimately to these classes' capacity to reproduce themselves.

Of course, we need not believe Freud, and we may very well suspect him of trying to elicit middle-class fears of downward mobility to expand the realm of action of psychoanalysis. Yet, his remarks contain very interesting sociological insights, especially his suggestion that parallel to the standard hierarchy of material and symbolic goods may run another emotional hierarchy which may disrupt and even run counter to the conventional hierarchy of privileges. But then, and this is the poignant irony of it all if you like, while there might have been a historical moment where, thanks to her emotional openness, the caretaker's daughter could succeed where the landlord's daughter would have failed, Freud and the therapeutic persuasion have created a world in which the landlord's daughter has, once again, far more advantages than the caretaker's daughter. These advantages are not only in the conventional socioeconomic sense that we know, but in the emotional sense as well. For, in having become a property of the middle-class workplace, the therapeutic ethos makes men and women far more ready and able to cope with the contradictions, tensions, and uncertainties that have become intrinsic to and structurally embedded in contemporary biographies and identities.[60] The landlord's daughter is now likely to have had a mother and a father very well versed in psychological methods of education, and is likely herself to have undergone therapy of some form, thus suggesting that she acquires the emotional habitus with which she will successfully compete in the marriage and economic marketplace. What this means for our understanding of the relationship between one's emotional life and social class remains to be examined, but it does suggest that capitalism has made us Rousseauian with a vengeance, not only in the sense that emotional fields of action have made identity publicly exposed and publicly narrated, not only in the sense that emotions have become instruments of social classification, but also in the sense that there are now new hierarchies of emotional well-being, understood as the capacity to achieve socially and historically situated forms of happiness and well-being.

3   Romantic Webs*

Let me start *in media res*, with a movie which was quite popular at the time it came out. Nora Ephron's 1999 movie *You've Got Mail* is the story of a children's bookshop owner – Kathleen Kelly – who has a boyfriend in real life but also has a platonic romance with someone on the net. She does not know her Internet friend, but we the viewers know who each one of the pair is. Thus, when Joe Fox (Tom Hanks), owner of a mega-bookstore à la Barnes and Noble, puts Kathleen Kelly (Meg Ryan) out of business, we the viewers know that these two enemies are in fact best romantic friends on the net. The movie unfolds following the genre of the "screwball comedy" as the two main protagonists throughout the movie act out their dislike, which turns into a reluctant attraction, to finally surrender to their mutual love. But what makes the movie an Internet romantic comedy is the fact that when faced with the choice between Joe Fox (to whom she has become attracted, and whom we know she likes) and her online lover, Meg Ryan chooses the latter (not knowing that they are one and the same). Of course, all ends happily when she finds out that her Internet lover and the person she has reluctantly become attracted to in real life are one and the same. The point of all this is simple: in the movie, the Internet self appears to be far more authentic, genuine, and compassionate than the social public self, more likely to be dominated by fear of others, defensiveness, and deceit. In contrast to the net romance, in the course of which both can reveal to each other their hidden weaknesses and true generosity, in "real life" both Joe Fox and Kathleen showed one another their worst – presumably false – self.

On the face of it, this is surprising. As one Internet researcher asks: "how [can] romantic interpersonal relationships . . . come to exist in this seemingly inanimate and impersonal global matrix of computers?"[1] The response given by the movie is simple: What makes the net romance so incontestably superior to real life relationships is the fact that the net romance annuls the body, thus presumably enabling a fuller expression of one's authentic self. Clearly, the Internet is presented as a disembodying technology and positively so, in the sense that the movie relies on the idea that the self is better revealed and more authentic when presented outside the constraints of bodily interactions. This idea is in turn congruent with a "central utopian discourse around computer technology" which centers on "the potential offered by computers for humans to escape the body. . . . In computer culture, embodiment is often represented as an unfortunate barrier to interaction with the pleasures of computing. . . . In cyber-writing, the body is often referred to as the 'meat,' the dead flesh that surrounds the active mind which constitutes the 'authentic' self."[2]

In this view then, the body – or rather, its absence – enables emotions to evolve from a more authentic self, and to flow toward a more worthy object, namely the disembodied true self of another. Yet if that is the case, from the standpoint of a sociology of emotions, this should pose a special problem because emotions in general and romantic love in particular are grounded in the body. Sweaty palms, quickening heart, reddening cheeks, shaking hands, clasped fists, tears, stuttering, these are only some of the examples of the ways in which the body is deeply involved in the experience of emotions, and of love in particular. If that is the case, and if the Internet annuls or brackets the body, how then can it shape, if at all, emotions? More exactly, how does technology rearticulate corporality and emotions?

Romancing the Internet

Internet dating sites have become highly popular and profitable enterprises. By 1999 one in 12 adult singles in the US had tried online matchmaking,[3] and the American match.com, established as early as 1995, claimed to have over five million registered users and today boasts 12 million visitors daily.[4] Exact data are not readily available, but it would seem that between 20 million and 40 million people in America alone look at online dating sites each month,[5] including over one million over-65s.[6] With monthly packages costing around $25, online dating is also a lucrative business. Indeed, by the third quarter of 2002 dating sites became the largest online paid content category, with revenues of over $300 million for the year. In the overall context of the Internet economy, online dating sites and ads are top Internet money makers, in the third quarter of 2002 taking a revenue of $87 million, a 387 percent increase over the same quarter in the previous year.[7]

In this lecture, I will be mostly interested in sites that claim to help people find long-term relationships; I am less interested in sites that have a more explicit sexual orientation, for the simple reason that I am precisely interested in the articulation of technology and emotions.[8]

Virtual meetings

How is one's self made to interact with an Internet dating site? How does one in fact get to meet virtual others? To be able to access the vast pool of available potential partners, numerous sites have customers complete a questionnaire called one's "profile." As one site boasts, "The objective is to give you additional tools to help define your emotional match and get beyond the mere physical."[9] On the very popular eHarmony.org website, the fastest growing Internet dating site, the questionnaire which will help build one's profile is not only designed by a psychologist but is patented as well. In other words, the Internet technology is predicated on an intensive use of psychological categories and assumptions about how to understand the self and how to engineer sociability through emotional compatibility. Thus, eHarmony boasts it is different from "anything you've experienced before. . . . Our Personality Profile . . . help[s] . . . you learn more about yourself and your ideal partner and allow[s] us to match you with highly compatible singles." The site was founded by a clinical psychologist, Dr Neil Clark Warren, who claims to have gathered scientific evidence enabling him to predict successful marriages (such as personality, lifestyle, emotional health, anger management, sexual passion, etc.). Once you have answered close to 500 questions, you are ready to pay your membership fees and launch a computer search for a compatible profile. The "profile" is thus the computer version of who you are. It is this psychological profile which will be matched with those of potentially compatible others.

Thus in order to meet a virtual other, the self is required to go through a vast process of reflexive self-observation, introspection, self-labeling, and articulation of tastes and opinions. For example, match.com makes one construct one's self through the following possible categories. The section on "your appearance" includes detailed descriptions of one's eyes (one is given eight possibilities to describe one's eye color), one's hair (13 possibilities, e.g. "braided," "buzzed," "wind-tossed," and "flipped"), the tattoos on one's body, and a category suggestively called "brag a little: what is your best feature?" (belly-button, legs, lips, etc.). The second category contains "my interests" with such subheadings as "What do you do for fun?," "What are your favorite local hotspots or travel destinations?," "Your favorite things," "How would you describe your sense of humor?," and "What kinds of sports and exercise do you enjoy?"; or a section such as "What common interests would you like to share with other members?" The section on lifestyle contains very detailed questions about one's diet, exercise routine, smoking habits, patterns of drinking, whether one has children or whether one wants them, whether one likes a wide variety of pets such as birds, cats, dogs, fish, exotic pets, fleas, gerbils. Another section deals with one's "values." This includes a detailed questionnaire about one's religious faith and practice, and one's political beliefs. Another section includes a series of questions about one's desired date (repeat of the questions about oneself regarding appearance, education, religion, politics, smoking and drinking habits, etc.). In addition, one can also find such questions as "What turns you

on and off?" (offering such possible answers as "body pierc-
ings," "long hair," "erotica," "money," "thunderstorms," or
"power").

In short, on Internet dating sites, one is simultaneously
asked to describe oneself objectively and to summon and
refine, in fantasy, one's ideals (of love, of a partner, and of lifestyle). Such processes of self-presentation and search for a
partner are entirely predicated on psychological persuasion in
at least three respects. First, the self is constructed by breaking
it down into discrete categories of tastes, opinion, personality,
and temperament, and is thus made to meet another on the
basis of the idea and ideology of psychological and emotional
compatibility. Meeting requires a great deal of introspection
and the capacity to articulate the psychological profile of
oneself and of another.

Second, the act of posting a profile allows the Internet, like
other psychological cultural forms such as talk shows and
support groups, to convert the private self into a public performance. More exactly, the Internet makes the private self visible
and publicly displayed to an abstract and anonymous audience,
which, however, is not a public (in the Habermasian sense of
that word) but rather an aggregation of private selves. On the
Internet, the *private psychological* self becomes a public
performance.

Finally, like much of the psychological persuasion, the
Internet contributes to a textualization of subjectivity (as discussed in lecture 1), that is, to a mode of self-apprehension in
which the self is externalized and objectified through visual
means of representations and language.

This in turn has four obvious consequences: in order to
meet another person, one is made to focus intensely on oneself,
on one's perception of one's own self, and on one's self-ideal
as well as one's ideal of another. One's sense of uniqueness
may thus be said to be sharpened by the Internet dating sites.
The second consequence is that the order in which romantic
interactions have been traditionally conducted is reversed: if
attraction usually precedes knowledge of another person, here
knowledge precedes attraction, or at least the physical presence
and embodiment of romantic interactions.[10] In the current

Internet situation, people are apprehended first as a set of attributes and only then do they apprehend – in incremental stages – the bodily presence of another.]

The third consequence is that the meeting is organized under the aegis of the liberal ideology of "choice." No technology I know of has radicalized in such an extreme way the notion of the self as a "chooser" and the idea that the romantic encounter should be the result of the best possible choice. That is, the virtual encounter is literally organized within the structure of the market.

Finally, the Internet places each person searching for another in a market in open competition with others. When you sign up to the site, you are immediately put in a position where you compete with others who are actually visible to you. The technology of the Internet thus positions the self in a contradictory way: it makes one take a deep turn inward, that is, it requires that one focus on one's self in order to capture and communicate its unique essence, in the form of tastes, opinions, fantasies, and emotional compatibility. On the other hand, the Internet also makes the self a commodity on public display. The process of searching for a partner through the Internet is simultaneously the conjunction of intense subjectivism – which takes a psychological form – and of an objectivization of the encounter, through technology and through the market structure of the site. This in turn represents a significant departure from the tradition of love. This is what I wish to explore next.)

Ontological self-presentation

Warren Susman viewed the beginning of the twentieth century as a turning point in the ways in which the self was negotiated and presented. Contrasting "personality" with "character," Susman suggests that, for the first time, the self became something to be assembled and manipulated for the sake of impression-making and impression management. In his view, consumer culture and fashion industry played an important role in accentuating the deliberate self-management and impression-making calculated to please and seduce another person. This marked an important change from the nine-teenth-century self which was less fragmented and less given to a context-dependent manipulation, because it was shaped by a holistic notion of character.

At face value, the Internet enables a far more flexible, open-ended, and multiple self, thus marking the epitome of the postmodern self in its capacity to make the self playful, self-inventing, and even deceitful in its capacity to manipulate information regarding the self.

However, the dating sites I am discussing differ from the postmodern uses of the Internet, precisely because they make the self apprehend itself through psychological tech-nologies of self. Indeed, a postmodern self consists chiefly in the self-conscious manipulations of one's body, speech patterns, manners, and clothing. The work of self-presenta-tion enacted in and by the Internet is of a different order, because it consists exclusively of language – and more spe-cifically written language – and because it is not geared to a specific, concrete other, but rather to a general audience of unknown, abstract candidates. In other words, the work of self-presentation of the postmodern self presupposes and entails the ability to be sensitive to different social contexts and to act different roles in them. In the case of the Internet dating sites, self-presentation takes an opposite character: it presupposes a movement inward toward one's most solid sense of self (who am I and what do I want?); it is general and standardized (one presents oneself through a standard questionnaire). It is not context- or person-sensitive in the sense that the purpose of the profile is to proffer one's truth about oneself, regardless of its reader's identity. The work of self-presentation becomes many steps removed from actual social performance and is performed both visually and lin-guistically not for a concrete, specific other, but for a gener-alized and abstract audience.

Whereas the postmodern self implies there is no core self, only a multiplicity of roles to be played, the self that is posited by the conjunction of psychology and the Internet technology is "ontic" in the sense that it assumes there is a core self which is permanent and which can be captured through a multiplicity of representations (questionnaire, photo, emailing) and so on. The Internet revives with a vengeance the old Cartesian dualism between mind and body, with the only real locus for thought and identity being in the mind. To have an Internet self is to have a Cartesian cogito, and to be involved in the world by looking at it from within the walls of one's consciousness.

The irony however is that in the process of self-presentation, physical appearance acquires a new and almost poignant importance in the photo usually posted near one's profile.

Despite the disembodying aspects of the Internet, beauty and the body are ever-present, but now, because they have become congealed, fixed images freezing the body in the eternal present of the photograph, and because this photograph is located in a competitive market of similar photographs, the Internet dating sites generate intense practices of bodily self-transformation. In fact, because the picture stands for the person, it has led many to engage in dramatic bodily changes. For example, one respondent, Sigal, a 20-year-old woman, claims that as a result of using the Internet she lost 20 kg (44 pounds) because she became aware of the fact that the photograph plays such an important role in the first selection. Or to take another example, Galia, a 30-year-old advertising executive, says: "This summer I wanted to upgrade my profile, so I went to my sister who has a good understanding of these things, and she said that she would help me improve how I look. So I went to the hairdresser, lost some weight, got new glasses, and re-did my pictures."

In presenting themselves through a photograph, individuals are literally put in the position of people who work in the beauty industry as models or actors, that is, they are put in a position (1) where they are made hyperconscious of their physical appearance, (2) where the body is the main source of social and economic value, (3) where through their body they are made to compete with others and, finally, (4) where their body and appearance are on public display. This reminds me of a footnote by Adorno and Horkheimer who, toward the end of the *Dialectic of Enlightenment*, offered a reflection relevant to this discussion. Discussing contemporary culture, they claim:

"The body is scorned and rejected as something inferior, and at the same time desired as something forbidden, objectified and alienated."[11]

The linguistic side of the profile puts one no less in a situation of intense competition with others, the problem being to break with the uniformity of the profiles. An example of this uniformity can be found in an analysis of the content of the little box which summarizes one's innermost self (located near the photo of the candidate). I looked at 100 such boxes. A surprising majority of them use the same adjectives to describe themselves. "I am a fun, outgoing, confident woman," or "I am cute and fun, newly single," "I am outgoing, full of life, and fun," "I am fun and adventurous," "OK, here it goes, I am fun, funny, short, brown-haired, brown-eyed, crazy," "I am an attractive, upbeat, fun 39-year-old woman who takes good care of those she loves," "Oh my – what do I say – fun loving, happy-go-lucky, hopeless romantic." I think that what is happening here is not very mysterious: The process of describing oneself draws from cultural scripts of the desirable personality. When presenting themselves in a disembodied way to others, people use established conventions of the desirable person and apply them to their selves. In other words, the use of written language for self-presentation creates, ironically, uniformity, standardization, and reification. I say "ironically" because when people are filling in these questionnaires they are meant to experience themselves and display to others their uniqueness.

This problem is well perceived by the writers of dating guidebooks. For example:

> Whether you're a man or a woman, if you sound like everyone else, it will be really hard for someone to come up with a way to write to you. How do you initiate conversation with a man when all he writes is that he wants a woman who's "kind, smart, funny, considerate, romantic, sexy, and athletic"? Well, I guess you could say "Hi. I'm kind, smart, funny, considerate, romantic, sexy, and athletic. I think we'd be a perfect match." I don't think so.[12]

The problem addressed here is the fact that, when mediated through language, self-presentation takes on a uniform character. The Internet thus creates reification, in the non-Marxist sense of the term, namely it makes people treat themselves and others as linguistic categories; it treats the abstract concept as if it were the real thing. This also connects with Lukács' definition of reification as "a relation between people [that] takes on the character of a thing and thus acquires a 'phantom objectivity', an autonomy that seems so strictly rational and all-embracing as to conceal every trace of its fundamental nature: the relation between people."[13] Indeed, such phantom objectivity, which subsumes the self under linguistic labels and social interaction under technology, haunts Internet dating sites.

To summarize: Where the most successful psychological profile demands that one stand out of the homogeneous pack of the "I am fun and funny," the photographic profile demands on the contrary that one fit established canons of beauty and fitness. Thus, the most successful people on the net are those who distinguish themselves by their linguistic originality and physical conventionality.

Standardization and repetition

Not only is self-presentation plagued by the problems of homogeneity and standardization, but the romantic encounter itself faces numerous such problems. These problems begin with the extremely long list of potential candidates one is faced with after defining one's desired partner. Although there are many criteria, they are nonetheless limited and, together with the huge databases the largest sites boast, it is not surprising that a typical search yields usually a large amount of potential candidates. For example, if you are looking for a blond, thin, non-smoker, below the age of 35, with a college education, unavoidably, a vast number of people will correspond to that description.

The sheer volume of interactions forces one to develop standard techniques of management and makes meetings both online and offline highly repetitive. Consider Artemis, a 33-year-old woman, who has been on the Internet for six years. Artemis is a technical translator and works at home. She uses the computer for her work and because she works at home she can in fact be constantly involved in the task of managing the large pool of men who are interested in her profile. Her card has been visited by 26,347 people and, as she says in her blog, "my profile is constantly visited and I also constantly visit other people's sites." In order to manage the large flow of virtual encounters, she has put the men on file on her computer, creating different folders for each of them, otherwise, as she puts it, "it is difficult to follow." The volume of interactions is so high that websites themselves have developed techniques and markers designed to help users cope with the large quantity of people, as hot lists, stars, peaches and trophies, and flames that read "hot." The law of numbers is crucial here and seems to have significantly changed the ways in which romantic life unfolds. As was the case in the realm of economic production at the turn of the twentieth century, people in the arena of romantic relationships now face the problem of knowing how to handle a much greater volume and speed of romantic "production," exchange, and consumption. For example, because of the sheer volume of interactions, many users send the same standardized message to all the people they are interested in, thus making the entire process akin to that of telemarketing. To take an example from a guidebook to Internet dating, "Alex even had a crib sheet with hometown, occupation, and college listings, so he could brush up on details before returning any calls."[14]

Because of the volume and frequency of encounters, the conversation and the meeting unavoidably take on a scripted character, with many interviewees mentioning the fact that they ask the same questions and tell the same jokes over and over again in the course of meeting their Internet dates. Writing about those meetings, Artemis, the woman we met before, writes in her blog:

> I know the rituals so well. It starts with the fact that I almost have a "uniform" for a blind date. It goes according to the period – to each period and season its uniform. Usually, I prefer jeans and a nice shirt, something I feel good about, physically and in terms of how good I feel about myself. . . . In most cases, I have no expectations and *don't get very excited*. I know exactly what will happen.

The volume of interactions makes actors rely on a limited repertoire of gestures and words which, when habitually repeated, quickly come to be viewed with a tired self-conscious irony. This is because much of the enchantment we have traditionally associated with the experience of romantic love is related to an economy of scarcity which in turn enables novelty and excitement.

By contrast, the spirit presiding over the Internet is that of an economy of abundance, where the self must choose and maximize its options and is forced to use techniques of cost–benefit and efficiency. This is glaringly obvious in a recent development in dating sites: a new form of Internet dating called speed-matching. This is how match.com advertises speed-matching: "Online speed-matching is a new, exciting way to date local singles online from your home, office, or on the go with your laptop. You'll see each date's photo and profile before talking live on the phone for four minutes." One is asked to choose from a list of sessions scheduled at fixed times, for example Sunday, October 6 at six o'clock. These sessions in fact correspond to marketing niches: examples of such sessions are "Jewish Singles," "Marriage Minded," "Catholic Singles," "Recently Divorced," "Travel Lovers," "Outdoors Lovers," "Fitness Enthusiasts," and so on. Once a niche is chosen, you register for a certain day and time where you will speak with six people for exactly four minutes each. Here the computer tries to mimic a live interaction as closely as possible by having people interact through voice and a photo posted while talking. While you speak with someone, the screen shows a clock ticking. When the four minutes are over, you are automatically disconnected. You are then requested to fill a "scorecard" with three categories, "yes," "no," or "maybe." You are then made to move to the next date and so on and so forth until you have finished the session of six virtual dates.

Speed-matching evolves from the obvious desire to maximize time and efficiency by targeting the population very precisely and by limiting the interaction to a strict and short time frame. This constitutes a perfect illustration of what Ben Agger calls "fast capitalism" which has two characteristics: first, capitalist technology tends to compress time in order to increase

economic efficiency; secondly, capitalism tends to erode boundaries and to deny people private space and time. In fast capitalism, the two characteristics are closely intertwined as
technology and commodity colonize time and space.[15]

The Internet technology fuses two main cultural logics or
ways of enlisting the self: that of psychology and that of consumerism. Using and relying on the logic of consumerism and
psychology, the Internet radicalizes the demand that one find
for oneself the best (economic and psychological) bargain.
More exactly, psychological categories are used to integrate
romantic encounters into the consumerist logic of increasingly
narrowing, defining, and refining tastes. Consumerism is
here enlisted to improve the quality of the (romantic) bargain
one will get. As a guidebook to Internet dating puts it, "the
more experience you have, the more refined your tastes and
the fewer people you may be willing to consider." [16] An example
of this is again Artemis, the woman we met earlier. "I am
looking for somebody, for something that does not exist but is
very, very specific. It has to be somebody brilliant, mostly in
the scientific domain. But somebody complex which is something I can see in their cards, but also in Instant Messaging.
They have to prove themselves in writing." Consistent with the
logic of consumer culture, the technology enables and even
encourages an increasing specification and refinement of
tastes. Contrary to needs, which are fixed, refinement is inherently unstable: for even the most gourmet of food can always
be surpassed. In the realm of dating, the process of refinement
has one important implication: the process of searching another
becomes inherently unstable – to be refined is precisely to look
for ways to improve one's position in the market.

Let me take two examples. First, Bruce, a 41-year-old computer software designer living in New York City:

> *Interviewer*: When going through profiles that may interest you,
> how exactly do you decide to get in touch with someone? I
> mean, let's say one of the women whose profile you're flipping
> through is good-looking but doesn't have exactly the kind of
> profession or education you would like, what do you do? Do
> you get in touch with her?

Bruce: No. There are so many choices, as I said before, infinite choices, that – uhmmm – why bother? I will get in touch only with those who correspond exactly to what I want.

My second example is Avi, a 27-year-old Israeli computer programmer who has been on the net for a few years and who, after using it intensively for many months, became increasingly disenchanted with it. He claims that the problem of the Internet is that people develop a strong desire for someone who is, as he puts it, "above their league," someone who is worth more than they themselves. People do not want to settle for someone who is comparable to them. But, rather, because they get to see from up close so many people who are above their league, and because the Internet gives them the illusion that they are easily within reach, then they will crave these people, not those they can get. And, he adds that, if a woman is interested in him, that makes her automatically suspect and contributes to inhibiting his interest and desire because, he says, he infers from that that he is above her league. In other words, Avi suggests that people look for the best value they can get, and in that process refine their tastes, and in fact refuse to settle for a bargain which they believe they can always improve on. The Internet enables such a process of bargaining in an unprecedented way for a simple reason: one actually visualizes the market of potential partners. Whereas in the real world, the market of partners remains virtual – never seen, only presupposed and latent – on the net, the market is real and literal, not virtual, because Internet users can actually visualize the market of potential partners.

Interestingly enough, the fact that Internet dating makes encounters into economic transactions is not lost on most users. In fact, economic metaphors and analogies have become widely pervasive in the offline meetings which follow Internet interactions. Most, if not all, of my interviewees in Israel and in the US mentioned that meeting someone requires them to "market themselves," and to perform as if in a job interview where they are alternately interviewee and interviewer. For example, Galia:

Interviewer: Have you ever used [an internet dating site]?

Galia: Unfortunately, yes.

Int: It sounds like you didn't like it much.

Galia: No, No, it's not the site. It's the dating I can't stand. Look, I'm a very sociable, extrovert person. I don't mind at all talking to people. But here you really have to do a sales pitch, you've got to present yourself the best possible way, you've got to interview quickly to find out what he is about. You've got to sell yourself in the best possible way, without knowing really who the person is, without knowing your target audience.

Int: What do you mean, "sales pitch"?

Galia: Basically you've got to sell yourself. I've no problem doing that but you have to face the fact that you have to do with. Because the only purpose of the meeting, of that conversation, is "do we want to keep seeing each other?" as a couple?

Int: How do you sell yourself?

Galia: Basically I am a very genuine person. But [when I am on these dates] I would smile a lot, be very, very, very nice, I do not express any extreme opinion, although my opinions are extreme and I am an extremist.

Int: Why then don't you enjoy the process?

Galia: I think I have missed an essential component of the whole thing. I really don't enjoy dating, all this dating. In 99 percent of cases I simply don't enjoy myself. I do it because I really want to meet someone and because I get tired of being alone. But I also get tired of meeting so many people, telling the same jokes, asking the same questions, having a painted smile on my face.

There is something new here. The Internet structures the search for a partner as a market or, more exactly, formalizes the search for a partner in the form of an economic transaction: it transforms the self into a packaged product competing with others on an open-ended market regulated by the law of supply and demand; it makes the encounter the outcome of a more or less stable set of preferences; it makes the process of searching constrained by the problem of efficiency; it structures encounters as market niches; it attaches a (more or less) fixed economic value to profiles (that is, persons) and makes people anxious about their value in such a structured market and eager to improve their position in that market. Finally, it makes people highly aware of the cost–benefit aspects of their search, both in terms of time, and in the sense that they want to maximize the attributes of the person found. These characteristics of the search are clearly felt, even if obscurely, by my respondents. Indeed, you will not have failed to notice that the interviews I have quoted so far contain a combination of tiredness and cynicism, a cynicism which was often the dominant tone of many other interviews as well. To follow up a suggestion offered by philosopher Stanley Cavell, I would say that tone is a matter of great importance, because it points to the overall emotional organization of experience. This cynicism marks a radical departure from the traditional culture of romanticism and is an effect of the routinization produced by the sheer volume of encounters and by the market structure and culture which pervades Internet dating sites. Cynicism is a particular structure of feeling which emerges from a property of consciousness and action particularly at work in late capitalist societies. I think that such cynicism is what Adorno had in mind when he suggested that in contemporary culture, consumers feel compelled to buy and use advertising products even though, and at the very moment, they see *through* them. Seeing through and obeying, Adorno tells us, is precisely the dominant mode of using consumer products in late capitalist societies. Cynicism is the tone one is likely to use when one sees through and yet feels compelled to do the same thing over and over again. This compulsion to "do" even though one "sees through" points to the fact that, to borrow a phrase from Žižek, "the illusion is not on the side of knowledge, it is already on the side of reality itself, of what people are doing."[17]

We thus have here a radical departure from the culture of love and romanticism which characterized much of the nineteenth and twentieth centuries. In their study of the cultural categories through which people make sense of "love at first sight,"[18] Schurmans and Dominicé suggest, on the basis of in-depth interviews with one hundred and fifty people, that the experience of *le coup de foudre* (love at first sight, literally in French "thunderbolt") contains a few recurring characteristics: it is experienced as a unique event, which erupts brutally and unexpectedly in one's life; it is inexplicable and irrational; it is put into motion immediately after the first encounter, and therefore, I may add, not based on any cognitive, cumulative knowledge of the other person. It disturbs one's daily life and operates as a deep commotion of the soul. The metaphors used are those of heat, magnet, thunder, electricity, all of which indicate a force that is overwhelming and overpowering. And I think that the Internet marks a radical departure from such a tradition of love.

Whereas romantic love has been characterized by an ideology of spontaneity, the Internet demands a rationalized mode of partner selection, which contradicts the idea of love as an unexpected epiphany, erupting in one's life against one's will and reason. Second, whereas traditional romantic love is intimately connected to sexual attraction – usually provoked by the presence of two physical, material bodies– the Internet is based on disembodied textual interaction. The result is that on the Internet, a rational search takes precedence, both in time and in approach, over traditional physical attraction. Third, romantic love presupposes disinterestedness, that is, a total separation between the sphere of instrumental action and the sphere of sentiment and emotion. Internet technology increases the instrumentalization of romantic interactions by placing a premium on the "value" people attribute to themselves and to others in a structured market. Love is irrational, by which it is meant that one does not need cognitive or empirical knowledge to know that this is the one and only. The Internet, on the other hand, makes cognitive knowledge of another precede one's sentiments in time and importance. Finally, the idea of romantic love has often been accompanied by the idea of the uniqueness of the person loved. Exclusivity is essential to the economy of scarcity that has presided over romantic passion. On the other hand, if the Internet has a spirit, it is that of abundance and interchangeability. This is because Internet dating has introduced to the realm of romantic encounters the principles of mass consumption based on an economy of abundance, endless choice, efficiency, rationalization, selective targeting, and standardization.

Clearly then, we are witnessing a major shift in the romantic sensibility. There even seems to be here a qualitative leap from the situation I described in *Consuming the Romantic Utopia*. In that book, I depicted a situation in which consumer capitalism exacerbated, rather than destroyed, key experiences of romance. Longing for "fun," the desire to experiment with new forms of sexual freedom and the search for emotional intimacy were systematically worked within the leisure industry, to the point where it became difficult to disentangle romantic feelings from consumer experience and thus, as I argued there, we could not presume that the realm of commodities debased the realm of sentiment. The situation I am describing here is qualitatively different. Romantic relations are not only organized within the market, but have themselves become commodities produced on an assembly line, to be consumed fast, efficiently, cheaply, and in great abundance. The result is that the vocabulary of emotions is now more exclusively dictated by the market.

In a way, it is as if the designers of Internet dating sites had read and applied, to the letter, the diagnosis of doom and gloom by critical theorists, such as Adorno or Horkheimer. Rationalization, instrumentalization, total administration, reification, fetishization, commodification, and Heideggerian "enframing" seemed to leap out of the data I had gathered. The Internet seems to bring the process of rationalization of emotions and love to levels not dreamed of by critical theorists.

And yet, however tempting and self-evident this critique, I would like to resist it. More specifically, I would like to resist what I call the paradigm of "pure critique." I hope you will forgive me for using here terms and arguments already used in my book, *Oprah Winfrey and the Glamour of Misery*. Since I did not find any reason to change my opinion on this, neither did I change its phrasing.[19]

Traditional critique, especially the kind I see quite often practiced in cultural studies, is characterized by what I suggest calling a "longing for purity." Indeed, if many cultural critics accord a great deal of importance to culture, it is because they view it as the realm within which we can (and ought to) articulate ideals of beauty, morality, and politics.

Pure critique subsumes culture in the political sphere and, because of that, it has become to a large extent the counting of the ways in which culture either emancipates or represses, delivers "trash" or "treasure," a position which in turn threatens to impoverish our analysis of culture. This is impoverishing because, to use Barbara Johnson's cogent words, critique ought to leave "room for surprise; . . . for someone or something to surprise you and say 'Stand aside, I want to speak.' "[20] For cultural texts and practices to surprise us, we need to stop reducing them to their ability (or inability) to deliver a clear political or moral stance on the world.

The second drawback of pure critique is that it usually demands nothing less than a *total* point of view: when I claim that a given cultural practice (television program, Internet technology, etc.) is noxious to the cause of, say, minorities or women, I make this claim from the standpoint of the economic, political, and domestic social spheres. In other words, this critique is achieved by assuming that one sphere (the cultural) both reflects and shapes other social spheres (the economic, the political, the domestic) and is functionally and dialectically related to them through a structurally deeper social logic. The assumption that culture ought to be analyzed from the standpoint of all social spheres and that it is to society what a part is to the whole is at the cornerstone of critical theory.

In contrast, I suggest that there is no direct continuity between social spheres and that they do not necessarily mirror one another. This means that we cannot know a priori how symbols and values will "behave" in the social, political, and economic spheres. This is essentially because of the famous problem of unintended effects brilliantly analyzed by Max Weber: principles of action, ideas, and values which emerge in one sphere (e.g., the religious) can give birth to something quite different from what they originally intended in another sphere (e.g., the economic). To put it more simply: what can be backwards in one sphere (e.g. the economic) can be progressive in another (e.g., the cultural) and vice versa.[21]

A third problem in predicating cultural analysis on political critique is that inasmuch as culture and politics use language in different ways, they will inevitably clash with each other. A politician is summoned to use language in a referential way, by referring to a realm of praxis in which roads are built and wars fought by taking a clear stand vis-à-vis "reality" (for example, a politician must say clearly whether he favors increasing or decreasing taxes). On the other hand, a poem or a movie are neither summoned to refer to reality nor can be held accountable for distorting it. In fact, a poem or a movie can do just that, that is, say two contradictory things at one and the same time (e.g., praise individualism and community, love and duty, etc.) without being held accountable for violating norms of communication. Moreover, a politician is summoned to tell the truth and to make valid claims (a politician might lie or err, of course, but will always be held accountable for doing so), while a poem or movie is impervious to truthfulness. We may criticize a movie for being too realistic or not enough, but it would hardly make any sense to criticize a movie or a novel for "lying" or for falling short of understanding inflation or unemployment. By the same token, it is not as straightforward as it seems to use political criteria to evaluate popular culture, for the simple reason that popular texts are often self-consciously and deliberately ambiguous, ironic, reflexive, self-contradictory, and paradoxical. All of these are properties of television, no less than of other cultural creations, and these in turn exceed the field of politics, at least as it is traditionally understood.[22] While it is indisputable that culture is an extension of our social relations – in its systematic silences, closures, and oppositions – it however cannot be wholly contained by and subsumed under the political.

There is a final problem in subsuming culture under politics: it has to do with the fact that it frequently condemns the critic to an Olympian distance, increasingly untenable in an era where cultural democracy reigns supreme. Adorno's rejection of jazz is only one of the most famous examples of such radical (and mistaken) detachment from the concrete experiences and meanings from which culture springs. Critique is most forceful when it moves away from Olympian purity and is grounded in a deep understanding of the concrete cultural practices of ordinary actors. Unavoidably, this entails a "compromise" with purity. But this compromise is all the more called for when in the era of late capitalism, whether by choice or by necessity, the critic of contemporary culture is condemned to be located within the very commodified arena he or she criticizes. In contradistinction to the nineteenth-century intellectual who could criticize capitalism and yet be located "somewhere" outside its reach, few contemporary critiques can be found outside the compass of capitalist institutions and organizations. This does not mean we should resign ourselves to accepting the domination of capitalism over all social spheres. But it implies that we develop strategies of interpretation that are as cunning as the market forces we want to oppose. Powerful critiques are those which derive from an intimate understanding of their object. Thus my point is emphatically not to dispose of critique, but rather to engage in a critique that does not become the "counting of the ways" in which culture promotes (or fails to promote) a given political agenda (equality, emancipation, or visibility).

In fact, this suggestion is consistent with the goals of critical theory itself whose method is immanent criticism, which "starts with the conceptual principles and standards of an object, and unfolds their implications and consequences." As David Held suggests, critique proceeds, so to speak, "from within and hopes to avoid, thereby, the charge that its concepts impose irrelevant criteria of evaluation of the object."[23] Unfortunately, such understanding of critical theory has not been sufficiently heeded; nor am I sure that Adorno himself always applied it.

A model of "immanent critique" has been best developed by political philosopher Michael Walzer who, in his thought-provoking *Spheres of Justice*,[24] claims that we should apply different principles of justice to different social spheres (say, the family or the market). This is because each sphere contains different kinds of goods (say, love or money) which must be distributed differently. Walzer has famously argued for different "spheres" of justice, that is, for the idea that different social spheres are animated by different principles to define what in them is valuable and how to distribute equitably the resources to reach those goods. In two later books, *The Company of*

Critics[25] and *Interpretation and Social Criticism*,[26] Walzer has extended the argument of *Spheres of Justice* to the activity of critique and has maintained that, in order to criticize a cultural practice, the cultural critic ought to use the moral criteria at work within the community (or social sphere) she or he is critiquing. In other words, Walzer suggests that the critic's moral evaluation be intimately connected to the principles of evaluation and moral criteria of the object being critiqued. In a similar vein, I suggest that we ought to develop criteria of evaluation that are as much as possible internal to the traditions, criteria and meanings of the object we analyze. I suggest calling this way of approaching social practices "impure critique," a kind of critique which tries to tread the fine line between those practices which further people's own desires and needs – however distasteful these may be to us – and those practices which clearly hamper them from attaining their goals. In a way, my suggestion is reminiscent of Latour's and Callon's methodology:[27] in the same way that they suggest we analyze, say, competing scientific theories without presuming to know the winners and the losers, I suggest we analyze the social without presuming to know in advance the emancipatory or the repressive, but rather that we make these emerge from a thick contextual understanding of social practices.

Fantasy and disappointment

Let me thus start my critique from the main problem reported by respondents and discussed by the Internet dating guidebooks I have read: the problem of disappointment. That is, despite the abundance of choice afforded by Internet dating sites, most respondents report a repeated feeling of disappointment. The typical scenario described goes as follows: you browse the list of potential partners (or you get an email from someone) and based upon the photo posted and the person's profile you decide to engage in an email correspondence. If all goes well, you typically starts fantasizing about a prospective date. Those feelings lead to a telephone conversation. Many, if not all, respondents reported that if they liked the voice of the person they spoke to, they could then develop quite strong feelings for that person, thus suggesting that imagination can be self-sustaining in its capacity to generate emotions.

If the telephone conversation also goes well, it can lead to an actual meeting, which is where, in the vast majority of cases, people experience great disappointment. The problem is so widespread that a guidebook to Internet dating has a section entitled "Getting Ready for Picture Shock." The section starts as follows: "If you think voice shock is bad, wait until you experience photo shock. Almost no one looks like his or her pictures . . . even if your site offers a short video to watch, you'll still be surprised."[28] And the next section is even entitled "Preparing a Course of Action in Case of Extreme Disappointment."[29] A banal explanation for this is to suggest that it is the result of inflated self-presentation, or of the disparity between one's unreasonably high expectations and a necessarily limited reality. The Internet technology would exacerbate a dimension of experience deemed to be distinctly modern, namely the disparity between one's expectations and one's experience. Koselleck[30] has even argued that modernity is characterized by the increasing distance between reality and aspiration.[31] But I think that this claim has been insufficiently analyzed and understood. What does it mean exactly to say that modern culture creates unrealistic expectations? Just how does it do that? And why do expectations have to be disappointed? What relationship must the real bear to fantasy for it to be so crushingly disappointing?

My argument is that imagination, or the culturally and institutionally organized deployment of fantasy, is not an abstract or universal activity of the mind. Rather, it has a cultural form, which in turn must be analyzed. In his celebrated *Imagined Communities*, Benedict Anderson comes close to this suggestion when he argues that ways of imagining communities differ not according to whether they are true or false but according to *their style*. Similarly, the kind of day-dreaming and imagination excited and elicited by the Internet have a particular style, which remains to be elucidated.

I argue that the style of imagination that is deployed in and by Internet dating sites must be understood in the context of a technology which disembodies encounters, makes them pure psychological events, and textualizes subjectivity.) To unravel this style and its connection to disembodiment, let me first proceed, *a contrario*, by analyzing what is involved in meeting another face to face, body to body.

First, Goffman suggests that when two people are co-present, they exchange two types of information: the one they give, and the one they "give off." Goffman suggests that in an actual encounter, it is the information people give off rather than that they freely give that is crucial. The information they give off, despite their best self so to speak, is very much dependent on the ways in which they use their body (voice, eyes, body posture, etc.), thus suggesting that much of our interactions are a sort of negotiation between what we consciously monitor and what we have no control over. In other words, if in bodily interactions there is a certain gap or lag between what we say, between how we want to present ourselves and what we have no control over, then this makes it more difficult to describe what is most important about ourselves in words, given that it is precisely that which we are not aware of which is most likely to make a significant impression on the person we meet. For example, Michele, a young woman working in a large corporation, describes one of her Internet dates as follows:

> *Michele:* There was this guy, we corresponded for a while, and then we decided to meet. I arrived at the café and we shook hands and I knew immediately this would not be it.
> *Interviewer:* You knew it immediately?
> *Michele:* Yes, immediately.
> *Interviewer:* How did you know immediately?
> *Michele:* By the way he shook my hand. There was something so soft and mushy about it, something which I really didn't like.

This woman interpreted this man's personality by metonymy through a small bodily gesture – how he shook her hand – that he could hardly have been aware of. This is further illuminated by the work of cognitive psychologist Timothy Wilson who has studied the non-conscious self as distinguished from the

Freudian unconscious. As he claims, "There is increasing evidence that people's constructed self bears little correspondence to their non-conscious self."[32] The non-conscious self constitutes the set of automatic responses to the world which we have little knowledge of and over which we can exert little control. This in turn means that people do not and probably cannot know themselves well, and that they do not really know which kind of persons will make them feel what. As Wilson says, we simply seem to be bad at understanding and predicting our emotional states. I would add that we are bad at doing that even though we seem to have accumulated so much psychological knowledge about ourselves.

Second, Goffman has suggested moreover that in a situation of physical co-presence, there arises a sense "that people are close enough to be perceived in whatever they are doing, including their experiencing of others, and close enough to be perceived in this sensing of being perceived."[33] This means that interaction is a subtle process of adjusting what we say or how we behave to the perceived co-presence of another. From this co-presence arises a special kind of mutuality. Goffman is referring here to a form of practical knowledge of sociability, which is incompatible with cognitive knowledge. The Internet disturbs the kind of semi-conscious adjustment we make in concrete interactions precisely in giving precedence to cognitive, text-based knowledge. Let me give one example of that. The author of a guidebook on dating recounts that he once had a client named Helen who "told him about a man who was interested in her in real life. She went and actually checked his dating profile and found out that she was three years older than his desired cutoff age. In other words, they would have never been able to meet on the Internet."[34] The Internet renders one of the central components of sociability far more difficult, namely our capacity to continuously negotiate *with ourselves* the terms on which we are willing to enter into a relationship with others. Because the Internet reifies our tastes and opinions, the success of a meeting will depend on its capacity to reproduce and correspond to the written text of pre-established preferences, thus preventing the kind of co-presence Goffman was referring to. For example, Olga, a 31-year-old strikingly attractive journalist living in California, admits she has used the Internet since 1999 without much success, by which she means that she met a number of men who disappointed her soon after meeting them. In the last few months, however, she has been in a serious relationship with a man, a scriptwriter from Hollywood whom she met on the Internet. I asked her to explain why it worked with this man and not with the others. She responded:

> With the others, there always was a sense of disappointment, as I explained before. The pictures never really looked like the people in person. But with him, with Thomas, I saw his picture and I thought, no way; there is no way somebody so good-looking would be on the Internet. I thought it was a prank or something. But when I met him, he actually looked better than his picture. And he was not even aware of how good he looks. He wasn't aware of it.

This response is interesting in two respects: one is that the reason why this man was able to succeed where the others had failed is because his live performance managed to mirror and in fact outdo his textual performance. And this might be because, as Olga tells us, he was not aware of his looks, thus making his performance in fact evade the cognitive and economic process of self-evaluation and self-presentation implied and required by the Internet.

Third, these remarks are particularly significant when we compare them to research on the experience of romantic attraction in social psychology. "In romantic beginnings, seemingly superficial appearances are what matter. The discovery that someone has a 'great personality' *seems* to matter very little." More exactly, in an experimental study of the causes of romantic attraction, adults and teenagers were asked to state explicitly and verbally what was most important for them in a date. Male respondents claimed that character traits such as "sincerity" or "affectional disposition" were more important than looks.[35] In the same experiment, the same men were later shown pictures of either homely or very attractive women and were given personality sketches of these women. Whether the same woman was alternatively presented as "untrustworthy," "anxious," or "boastful" seemed to make little difference when compared to cases where the same woman was described as "trustworthy," "relaxed," or "modest." Attractive women were always found to be preferred to homely women, regardless of their character. This experiment thus suggests two important findings: one is that in general people think personality is important, when in fact personality attributes play very little role in interpersonal attraction. "[A]ttractiveness is exceedingly important. We are aroused by others who are physically and personally appealing."[36]

Another implication is that, despite their best efforts to control their attraction to a potential partner, people in fact just don't know what will make them attracted to someone else. In that respect, we may invoke here Merleau-Ponty's critique of the empiricist approach to perception of the phenomenal. He argues that the empiricist empties perception and feeling (sentir) of what he calls its "mystery." Merleau-Ponty distinguishes between sentir and connaître, where the latter refers to an apprehension of the object based on properties, or what Merleau-Ponty views as dead qualities of the object (qualités mortes). Feeling, on the other hand, refers to an experience of the active properties of the object. To see a motionless body is not the same as seeing a moving body. What is forgotten when perception is treated as an act of knowing, Merleau-Ponty claims, is the "existential background." Bourdieu, reviving Merleau-Ponty, employs a similar argument by putting the body squarely at the center of social interactions: "[A]fter two hundred years of pervasive Platonism, it is hard for us to think that the body can 'think itself' through a logic alien to the act of theoretical reflection."[37] This is because, Bourdieu suggests, social experience is accumulated and displayed in the body. Thus physical attraction, far from being irrational or superficial, activates mechanisms of recognition of social similarity precisely because the body is the repository of social experience. Thus, contrary to the psychological disembodied techniques for knowing oneself and others, it turns out that the body might be the best and perhaps only way to know another person and be attracted to them.

In fact, let me go back to the movie *You've Got Mail* and ask again what it is that makes the Internet couple work so well. As I stated earlier, this movie belongs to the genre of the "screwball" comedy, a genre which pitches men against women and unites or reunites them after it has made them enemies. The essence of the screwball romantic comedy is that, despite their enmity, the protagonists are nonetheless irresistibly attracted to each other. Indeed, undeniably what holds the movie together is the tension that builds up between Tom Hanks and Meg Ryan, a tension we know to be, in the tradition of the screwball romantic comedy, conducive to and even synonymous with attraction. In fact, when Ryan (Kathleen) and her regular boyfriend break up, they are both surprised that they in fact do not love each other, although they are "so perfect for each other." In contrast, although everything seems to divide Meg Ryan and Tom Hanks – especially the fact they are in business competition with each other and that Hanks crushes Ryan's lovely children's bookstore – their enmity hides and perhaps even generates a real attraction. In other words, at the same time that this movie portrays positively a new kind of disembodied love, based on self-revelation, a rational monitoring of the relationship, and elective affinity through a disembodied technology, its narrative conventions subscribe to, display, and enact an opposite conception of love, based on an irresistible and irrational attraction in which the body, the co-presence of two physical persons, is essential to the sentiment of love. In the screwball comedy, as in the best romantic tradition, love erupts precisely despite the conscious cogito of the protagonists. Moreover, when the Internet pen pals do meet, given that Meg Ryan and Tom Hanks are already in love, their cognitive knowledge of each other does not play any role at all in their final mutual declaration of love: bodily attraction – and not the Internet emotional affinity – has already done the volatile work of falling in love. So, the Internet romance turns out to be a fairly traditional romance after all where the knowledge the protagonists have accumulated of each other prior to their meeting plays a very small role. Moreover, I doubt very much that Meg Ryan's character would have liked Tom Hanks' half as much if she had never met him in real life. In the movie, as in real life, what does the work of romantic (and therefore social) attraction is the body.

Let me thus go back to the question with which I started the section, namely, what characterizes the kind of imagination that is deployed on the Internet; why has it such affinity with disappointment and what role does disembodiment play in disappointment? Love has always been deemed to put into motion imaginary scenarios which endow its object with mystery and power. Contrary to conventional wisdom, such imagination, far from being disconnected from reality, is on the contrary often triggered by a gesture, a way of moving and carrying one's body in the world. As Ethel Spector Person, a psychoanalyst who has spent some time observing how patients talk about love, says "[I]t may be the way someone lights a cigarette in the wind, tosses her hair back, or talks on the phone (I personally think such gestures 'tell' much, if not all, about the personality and aspirations of the person who is so observed . . ."[38] In other words, insignificant bodily gestures can and do trigger romantic fantasies and sentiments. Freud, reviving Plato, views such capacity to be moved by inexplicable and seemingly irrational details as the result of the fact that in love we love a lost object. "The enormous power the beloved seems to exert on the lover can in part be explained by the love object having been invested with the mystique of all the lost objects from the past."[39] In other words, in the particular cultural configuration Freud was working in, love and fantasy were closely intertwined through their capacity to mix past and present experiences in concrete, embodied interactions.

In this view, imagination is the capacity to substitute for the "real" experience of the real object by feeling sensations which are close to what they would be in real life. Imagination thus does not annul reality but on the contrary leans on it because it relies on sensations, feelings, and emotions to make present that which is absent. Traditional romantic imagination, because it is based in the body, synthesizes experience, mixes and combines the present object with images and experiences located in the past, and focuses on a few "revealing" details about the other. Moreover, for the pre-Internet romantic subject, love triggered imagination through processes of idealization.

To love was to over-evaluate, that is, to attribute to a (real) other an added value. It was the act of idealization which made the other person unique.[40] Thus in traditional love, imagination is generated through four basic processes: an attraction that is based in the body; such attraction mobilizes the subject's past relationships and experiences (where Freud understood these past experiences to be strictly psychological and biographical, we may view them, with Bourdieu, as social and collective); this process in turn takes place at the semi-conscious or unconscious level, thus bypassing the rational cogito; finally, traditional love almost by definition idealizes the other, that is, attributes to the beloved person a value often superior to ours. Such idealization often takes place through a combination of what we know and do not know about another.

We may explain love's capacity to mobilize the self in this way by invoking the Bourdieusian paradigm which stipulates that to love another is to recognize (and therefore to love) one's own past and one's social destiny, and social destiny is, according to Bourdieu, nowhere more apparent than in the body and when falling in love. To love is to recognize libidinously and in someone else's body our social past and our social aspirations.

Recent research in cognitive psychology on processes of decision making confirm the Bourdieusian view and has established the existence of "intuitive thinking," or what cognitive psychologists call "thin slicing," the ability to make accurate snap judgments about people, problems, and situations. Such snap judgments derive from unconscious thought processes, the capacity to mobilize past experiences and to zero in and focus on a very few elements of the object being judged. In falling in love, we identify or rediscover the people we have accumulated in the past and focus on a few details, thus forming a holistic view of the other and not a fragmented, check-box one. Cognitive psychologists would view the traditional model of love and its focus on the body not as a failure of judgment, but rather as the most efficient and quickest route for our mind to make such a decision.

In this cultural, social, and cognitive configuration – that of traditional love – the problem of falling in love is to enable the passage of spontaneous and seemingly irrational love to one sustainable in everyday life. On the other hand, the Internet imagination poses an altogether different problem, which I would summarize like this: it unleashes fantasy yet inhibits romantic feelings. The Internet imagination is triggered by two sets of texts, the photo and the profile, and by the knowledge of the other person that is verbal and rational, that is, based on categories and cognitions, not in the senses. The Internet imagination is triggered by a set of attributes which are not attached to a specific person, but rather are the outcome of one's own projection of another. As a guidebook to dating puts it: "Close your eyes for a moment. Make a mental picture of her. How old is she? How tall is she? What color are her hair and eyes? What kind of shape is she in? And, perhaps more important than her physical attributes, what kind of personality does she have?"[41] The process of fantasizing and of looking for someone is the process of defining a list of abstract and disembodied attributes prior to an actual encounter – in turn supposed to correspond to one's desired ideal, based on one's knowledge of one's needs and own personality attributes. Contrary to the romantic imagination that was body-based and which was of the order of what Merleau-Ponty called *sentir*, the Internet imagination is of the order of *connaître* which empties perception of its existential background.

The Internet provides a kind of knowledge which, because it is disembedded and disconnected from a contextual and practical knowledge of the other person, cannot be used to make sense of the person as a whole. In the movie *Love in the Afternoon* (Billy Wilder), Audrey Hepburn says to the man she is in love with (Gary Cooper) that she is "too thin," has too long a neck, has too big ears, to which he replies: "That may be, but I like the way it all hangs together." Face-to-face encounters cannot be reducible to a set of attributes; rather, they are "holistic," that is, in them we attend to the interconnectedness between a wide variety of attributes, rather than to each discrete attribute. What we commonly call the "charm" or "charisma" of another person consists precisely in the ways in which various attributes are integrated with each other and contextually performed. As Husserl has taught us, things have a relation to other things because they are grasped by "a perceiving and moving body."[42] When it is in touch with the world, the lived body has a reflexive experience, something Husserl calls *Empfindnisse*:

> [A] lived experience [*Erlebnis*] that is not an experience-of [*Erfahrung*], a sensorial event [*Empfindung*] that is not a perception [*Wahrnehmung*], a finding of oneself [*sich befinden*] that is not a finding of something. *Empfindnisse* are those peculiar sensorial events that . . . arise at the intersection of tactile sensations and kinaesthetic sensations and, at precisely that juncture where all distance is traversed, undergird the flesh of things with the flesh of the lived-body.[43]

I am not a Husserl specialist, but I would venture to suggest that love occurs in this particular way of encountering the world. This is why we often fall in love with people who are very far from our prior notions, or why, when in love, we are willing to disregard an element which does not match our expectations, precisely because we attend to the whole, rather than to its parts.

Let me say this differently by drawing again on the theoretical tradition of cognitive psychology and research on decision making. Some very interesting research done by the cognitive psychologist Jonathan W. Schooler[44] shows that when people are asked to remember a face in their minds and then identify this face in a line-up, they do quite well. However, if these people are asked first to describe the face in words and then to identify it, they actually do rather less well. Schooler calls this effect "verbal overshadowing," an interference of verbal processes with visual ones. Verbal processes are especially likely to interfere with those decisions which require us to use "our intuition," "insight," or snap judgment. In other words, there are things that we simply do better without words, that is, without verbalizing what it is that we are doing and why we are doing it. Moreover, not only do words interfere with snap judgments, but information overload actually diminishes rather than increases the capacity to make the kind of quick decision which defines romantic attraction.[45] Snap judgments use a type of cognition which is "fast and frugal," that is, minimal and which relies on the "signature" of a person or phenomenon, that is, on its barest elements. To give you an example of what is meant here: Experiments have shown that when you sell six kinds of jams, 30 percent of all people who stop by the booth are likely to buy a jam;[46] when you put 24 different kinds of jam in your booth, only 3 percent are likely to buy any kind of jam. The reason is simple: the greater the choice, the greater the risk of information overload, which in turn interferes with the capacity to make snap judgments based on little rather than lots of information.

Internet imagination is thus not opposed to reality; it is opposed to a kind of imagination that is based on the body and on intuitive thought (or "thin slicing").[47] The Internet imagination undercuts intuitive imagination because it is not retrospective, but prospective, that is, forward looking, and therefore disconnected from one's intuitive, practical, and tacit past knowledge. Moreover, because it relies on a mass of text-based cognitive knowledge, it is dominated by verbal overshadowing, a prevalence of language which interferes with processes of visual and bodily recognition. Finally, I would add that because the Internet makes us see the whole market of possible choices available to us (crudely put: it enables price shopping), in the actual encounter, we will usually tend to undervalue, not overvalue, the person encountered.

Where traditional romantic imagination is characterized by a mix of reality and imagination, both based in the body and in its past accumulated experience, the Internet splits imagination – as a world of self-generated subjective meanings – and the encounter with another, by having the two happen at different points of time. The knowledge of another is also many times split, for a person is apprehended first as a self-constructed psychological entity, then as a voice, and only later as a moving and acting body.

Such a particular form of imagination is for philosopher Merleau-Ponty a source of pathology. Indeed, for Merleau-Ponty, the imaginary and the real cannot be separated from each other and, as he suggests, it is the attempt to separate the two that constitutes pathology.[48]

Having said all that, how then do we explain that relationships do get formed on the net? Match.com boasts 9,000 marriages, and while this is undoubtedly a small fraction of the total number of people who use the net, a good analysis should still try to make sense of it and more generally of the meaningful bonds that are formed on and through the Internet.

Let me go back to Artemis, by far the choosiest respondent I interviewed. I asked her why a certain man she met on the net had interested her. She answered: "He related to my card. . . . People who interest me are those with great emotional competence. I need someone who will be able to relate to the emotional aspect of who I am. For example in my profile I wrote 'I have no patience for most people.' I need someone to relate to that, to try and understand where it comes from, why I wrote this."

The Internet is a supremely psychological technology, in the sense that it presupposes a psychological understanding of the self, and encourages a psychological mode of sociability. This is confirmed, perhaps unwittingly, by a large study of the relations formed on the net by social psychologists McKenna Green, and Gleason, who argue that people can and do form meaningful bonds on the net because it enables the expression of what they call the "authentic self."[49] To define the authentic self, they use none other than Carl Rogers's definition as being a kind of self which is often hidden from oneself and others and is best expressed in the therapeutic encounter. The researchers here merely reconfirm the reigning language ideology of psychology.

Let me thus surmise that it is those people who put a special premium on emotional verbal communication, those who are most competent at building a private relationship through public manipulation of their emotions and self, and at building relationships following the therapeutic model, those who display what I have called in my previous lecture emotional competence, who are most likely to maximize the technology of the Internet, thus making the Internet a truly psychological technology.

Conclusion: A new Machiavellian move

We have come full circle. Throughout the twentieth century, psychology became what Castoriadis calls "a magma" of social imaginary significations: by magma, Castoriadis means that it is an imaginary form that permeates all society, which unites it and which cannot be reduced to its components. The cultural imaginary of psychology has become our contemporary "magma." Its meanings are collectively shared and constitute our sense of self and our way of connecting to others.

Psychoanalysis was born from the withdrawal of the self into the private sphere and from the saturation of the private sphere with emotions. But in conjunction with the language of productivity and the commodification of selfhood in the field of mental health, the psychological persuasion has made the emotional self into a public text and performance in a variety of social sites such as the family, the corporation, support groups, television talk shows, and the Internet. The transformation of the public sphere into an arena for the exposition of private life, emotions, and intimacies which has characterized it for the last twenty years cannot be understood without acknowledging the role of psychology in converting private experiences into public discussion. The Internet is the latest development in this process, as it presupposes a psychological self which can apprehend itself through texts, classify and quantify itself, and present and perform itself publicly, its problem being precisely how to convert that public psychological performance back into a private emotional relationship.

Thus, as Adorno had so powerfully suggested more than half a century ago, disparate institutions are tightly linked together in a process of commodification of selfhood: the psychological persuasion, the self-help literature, the advice industry, the state, the pharmaceutical industries, the Internet technology are all intertwined to form the substrate of modern psychological selfhood because all of them have the self as their prime target. It is this progressive fusion of the market repertoires and languages of the self during the twentieth century which I have called "emotional capitalism." In the culture of emotional capitalism, emotions have become entities to be evaluated, inspected, discussed, bargained, quantified, and commodified. In this process of inventing and deploying a wide battery and range of texts and classifications to manage and change the self, they have also contributed to creating a suffering self, that is, an identity organized and defined by its psychic lacks and deficiencies, which is incorporated back into the market through incessant injunctions to self-change and self-realization. Conversely, emotional capitalism has imbued economic transactions – in fact most social relationships – with an unprecedented cultural attention to the linguistic management of emotions, making them the focus of strategies of dialogue, recognition, intimacy, and self-emancipation.

It is here that I stray from the legacy of critical theory and from what has become a conventional Foucaultian account of this process. The dynamic which has drawn a straight line from the Freudian imagination to the Internet is not one of total administration or surveillance because it is fraught with ambivalence and contradiction, for it is the same language and techniques which make relationships accountable and open to scrutiny that have also made possible the commodification of selfhood. In the process I have described, it is virtually impossible to distinguish the rationalization and commodification of selfhood from the capacity of the self to shape and help itself and to engage in deliberation and communication with others. It is the same logic which has made emotions into a new form of capital, which has also made relationships inside the corporation more accountable. It is the same cultural formation which has made women demand an equal position in the public and private spheres that has also made intimate bonds dispassionate, rationalized, and susceptible to crass utilitarianism. It is the same knowledge system which aimed at making us peek into the dark corners of our psyche and emotionally "literate" which has contributed to making relationships quantifiable and fungible entities. In fact, the very idea of "self-realization" – which contained and still contains a psychological and political *promesse de bonheur* – was central to the deployment of psychology as an authoritarian knowledge system and to the penetration of market repertoires inside the private sphere.

In the face of such perplexing intertwining of contradictory processes of rationalization and emancipation, of interests and passions, of private concerns and public repertoires, Foucault and a wide range of critical theorists, I think, would be happy to collapse these contradictions under such all-embracing processes as "commodification," or "surveillance," and to subsume pleasure under power. Postmodern sociologists, also, are unfazed by such states of affairs as they celebrate ambivalence and indeterminacy. Yet if there is anything I would like to claim forcefully at the end of these lectures, it is that even if the rationalization and commodification of selfhood remain irrevocably fused with its emancipation, we cannot confuse one with the other. Our task remains not to confuse power for pleasure. Yet, even as we strive for clarity, our analysis is inevitably messy, because it must cope with social spheres and values that are irrevocably intertwined with each other. If sociology has traditionally called on us to exert our shrewdness and vigilance in the art of making distinctions (between use value and exchange value; lifeworld and colonization of the lifeworld, etc.), the challenge that awaits us is to exercise the same vigilance in a social world which consistently defeats these distinctions.[50] To use again Michael Walzer's metaphor, the task of the critic should become akin to Hamlet's gesture to his mother when he gives her the glass to see herself as she really is in the innermost corners of her heart. "The task of the critic . . . is no different, for the glass he or she raises appeals to values and ideals that all of us spontaneously agree with and which we ourselves invoke to make other people accountable for their actions."[51] In raising such a glass, we are bound to see a blurred image indeed.

It is from this position that I have tried to examine the ambivalent logic tying emotions to capital. And it is also from this position and only from this position that I wonder if the ambivalent logic I traced throughout the twentieth century is not becoming more univocally shaped by the market. Indeed, if the conventional capitalist subject could shift back and forth from the "strategic" to the purely "emotional," in the era of psychology and the Internet, the main cultural problem, it seems to me, is that it becomes far more difficult to shift from the strategic back to the emotional. Actors seem to be stuck, often against their will, in the strategic. The Internet provides a striking example of this. It is not so much that Internet technology impoverishes personal and emotional life, but rather that it creates unprecedented possibilities for sociability and relationships but empties them of the emotional and bodily resources which have until now helped them carry on.

Discussing Simmel's theory of work, the sociologist Jorge Arditi helps us understand what is at stake here.[52] According to Arditi, Simmel formulated a theory of alienation under which the gradual impoverishment of personal life is a consequence of the growing separation between objective and subjective culture, between our experience and the world of objects and ideas produced outside us. As explained by Arditi, for Simmel, when we create a complex objective culture, we lose the unity needed for it to be meaningful. That is, for Simmel an object is existentially meaningful when subject and object are congruent. In this respect, Arditi suggests that to love means to apprehend the other directly and entirely. It means that no social or cultural object lies between the lover and the beloved, that is, that no element of the intellect plays any part in the experience of loving. These are well-known romantic ideas but I don't think they should be dismissed just because they are romantic. When we love someone, we attach to that person a meaning that derives from experiencing him or her as a whole. Intellectual experience – what Weber viewed as the essence of rationality – thus necessarily introduces a distance between oneself and the object. For Simmel, rationalization has brought about a significant increase in the distance between subject and object. And here Arditi offers a very interesting idea, namely that social distance derives not from the absence of common traits, but from the abstract nature of these traits. Remoteness, that is, does not set in because people have nothing in common, but because the things they have in common are, or have become, too common. To put this slightly differently, I would suggest that remoteness derives from the fact that people now share a common and highly standardized language. Conversely, closeness results from the specificity and exclusivity of similarities shared between two entities. In this sense, nearness implies the sharing of "existentially generated meanings." It is, in other words, the fact that, to an increasing degree, we have cultural techniques to standardize intimate relationships, to talk about them and manage them in a generalized way, which weakens our capacity for nearness, the congruence between subject and object.

I believe we are witnessing here a new cultural configuration, perhaps equivalent to the momentous rupture effected by Niccolò Machiavelli. As you may remember, Machiavelli argued that public conduct and success were to be kept separate from private morality and virtue and that the good leader ought to know how to calculate his moves and manipulate his persona in such a way as to appear generous, honest, and compassionate (all the while being thrifty, cunning, and cruel). Machiavelli was perhaps the first to formulate the essence of modern selfhood, namely its capacity to be split between the private and public realms of action, to distinguish and separate morality and self-interest and to shift back and forth from one to the other. The psychological persuasion has transformed the terms of this duality between a private moral self and a public amoral instrumental strategic conduct. For, through the cultural medium of psychology, the private and public spheres have become intertwined with each other, each mirroring the other, absorbing each other's mode of action and justification, and ensuring that instrumental reason be used in and applied to the realm of emotions and, conversely, making self-realization and the claim to a full emotional life become the compass of instrumental reason.

Does this state of affairs make us smarter and more able to achieve our aims? Machiavelli's Prince may not have enjoyed the approval of the moral authorities of his time, but he was at least supposed to be more skillful in the conduct of ordinary affairs. I have my doubts. Let me explain what I mean by referring to the fascinating research by neurologist Antonio Damasio who examined patients whose ventromedial prefrontal cortex (behind the nose) was damaged. According to neurologists, this is the area that is critical in the process of decision making. People with such damage are typically and perfectly rational, but they lack judgment and the capacity to make decisions based on emotion and intuition (intuition being understood here as nothing but accumulated cultural and social experience). This is how, in his book *Descartes' Error*, Damasio describes the process of trying to make an appointment with a patient with such brain damage:

> I suggested two alternative dates, both in the coming month and just a few days apart from each other. The patient pulled out his appointment book and began consulting the calendar. The behavior that ensued, which was witnessed by several investigators, was remarkable. For the better part of a half hour, the patient enumerated reasons for and against each of the two dates: previous engagements, proximity to other engagements, possible meteorological conditions, virtually anything that one could think about concerning a simple date. [He was] walking us through a tiresome cost–benefit analysis, an endless outlining and fruitless comparison of options and possible consequences. It took enormous discipline to listen to all of this without pounding on the table and telling him to stop.[53]

This man, trying to decide rationally when to have his appointment, is what I would call a hyperrational fool, somebody whose capacity to judge, to act and ultimately to choose is damaged by a cost–benefit analysis, a rational weighing of options that spins out of control.

Damasio's anecdote is, of course, a literal one, but we can use it in a metaphorical way to interpret all that I have been discussing in the last three lectures: I wonder if the process which I have been describing does not have this quality of making us hyperrational fools. As I have tried to suggest, we are increasingly split between a hyperrationality which has commodified and rationalized the self, and a private world increasingly dominated by self-generated fantasies. If ideology is what makes us live within contradictions with pleasure, I am not sure that the ideology of capitalism is able to do that any more. Capitalist culture may have reached a new stage: while industrial and even advanced capitalism enabled and demanded a split self, shifting smoothly from the realm of strategic to domestic interactions, from the economic to the emotional, from the selfish to the cooperative – the internal logic of contemporary capitalist culture is different: not only is the cost–benefit cultural repertoire of the market now used in virtually all private and domestic interactions but it is also as if it has become increasingly difficult to switch from one register of action (the economic) to another (the romantic). The dominance of hyperrationality in turn affects the very capacity to fantasize. Discussing Stanley Kubrick's last movie, *Eyes Wide Shut*, Žižek says "it's not that fantasy is a potent abyss of seduction that threatens to swallow you but quite the opposite: that fantasy is ultimately sterile."[54] Fantasies have never been as abundant and multiple in a culture which incessantly engineers them yet they may have become sterile because they are becoming disconnected from reality, and increasingly organized within the hyperrational world of choice and information about the market.

Notes

Chapter 1 The Rise of *Homo Sentimentalis*

1 Weber, Max, 1958, *The Protestant Ethic and the Spirit of Capitalism*, New York: Charles Scribner's Sons.
2 See Marx, Karl, 1904, "Estranged Labor," in Dirk J. Struik (ed.), *The Economic and Philosophic Manuscripts of 1844*, New York: Inter-national Publishing.
3 Simmel, Georg, 1950, "The Metropolis and Mental Life," in K. Wolff (ed.), *The Sociology of Georg Simmel*, New York: Free Press.
4 Durkheim, Emile, 1969, *Elementary Forms of Religious Life*, New York: Free Press.
5 Durkheim, Emile and Marcel Mauss, 1963, *Primitive Classification*. London: Cohen & West.
6 Durkheim, Emile, 1964, *The Division of Labor in Society*, New York: Free Press.
7 Of course, emotions do not play the same role in different sociological frameworks; but my point is that they do play a role.
8 McCarthy, Doyle E., 1994, "The Social Construction of Emotions: New Directions from Culture Theory," *Social Perspectives on Emotion* 2: 267–79.
9 McCarthy, Doyle E., 2002, "The Emotions: Senses of the Modern Self," *Osterreichische Zeitschrift für Soziologie* 27: 30–49.
10 Nussbaum, Martha C., 2001, *Upheavals of Thought: The Intelligence of Emotions*, Cambridge: Cambridge University Press.
11 Rosaldo, M., 1984, "Toward an Anthropology of Self and Feeling," in R. Schweder and R. LeVine (eds.), *Culture Theory: Essays in Mind, Self, and Emotion*, Cambridge: Cambridge University Press, pp. 136–57.

12   Abu-Lughod, Lila and Catherine A. Lutz, 1990, "Introduction: Emotion, Discourse, and the Politics of Everyday Life," in Catherine A. Lutz and Lila Abu-Lughod (eds.), *Language and the Politics of Emotion*, Cambridge: Cambridge University Press, pp. 1–23; Shields, Stephanie, Keith Oatley and Antony Manstead, 2002, *Speaking from the Heart: Gender and the Social Meaning of Emotion*, Cambridge: Cambridge University Press.

13   Coontz, Stephanie, 1988, *The Social Origins of Private Life: A History of American Families, 1600–1900*, New York: Verso Books. See Bellah, R., R. Madsen, W. Sullivan, A. Swidler, and S. Tipson, 1985, *Habits of the Heart: Individualism and Commitment in American Life*, Berkeley: University of California Press; or Lasch, C., 1984, *The Minimal Self: Psychic Survival in Troubled Times*, New York: W. W. Norton, for classical examples of such positions.

14   See Zelizer, Viviana, 1994, *The Social Meaning of Money*, New York: Basic Books.

15   Chertok, Leon and Raymond de Saussure, 1979, *The Therapeutic Revolution: From Mesmer to Freud*, New York: Brunner/Mazel Publishers; Ellenberger, Henry F., 1970, *The Discovery of the Unconscious: The History and Evolution of Dynamic Psychiatry*, New York: Basic Books.

16   Langer, Susanne K., 1976, *Philosophy in a New Key: A Study in the Symbolism of Reason, Rite, and Art*, Cambridge, MA: Harvard University Press, p. 3.

17   This discussion is based on Martin Albrow's "The Application of the Weberian Concept of Rationalization to Contemporary Conditions," in S. Lash and S. Whimster (eds.), 1987, *Max Weber: Rationality and Modernity*, London: Allen and Unwin, 164–82.

18   Habermas, J., 1989, "Self-Reflection as Science: Freud's Psychoanalytic Critique of Meaning," in S. Seidman, *Jürgen Habermas on Society and Politics: A Reader*, Beacon Press: Boston, p. 55. Habermas's claim is not universally accepted. For example, Henri Ellenberger claims that Freud was only one link in a long chain of psychotherapeutic treatments. See Ellenberger, *The Discovery of the Unconscious*.

19   Bellah, Robert, 1968, *Beyond Belief: Essays on Religion in a Post-Traditional World*, New York: Harper & Row, p. 67.

20   Anderson, Benedict, 1991, *Imagined Communities: Reflections on the Origin and Spread of Nationalism*, London: Verso.

21 Cavell, Stanley, 1996, "The Ordinary as the Uneventful," in Stephen Mulhall (ed.), *The Cavell Reader*, Oxford: Blackwell Publishers, pp. 253–9.

22 Freud, Sigmund, 1948, *Psychopathology of Everyday Life*, New York: Macmillan.

23 Taylor, Charles, 1989, *Sources of the Self: The Making of the Modern Identity*, Cambridge, MA: Harvard University Press.

24 Peter Gay, 1988, *Freud: A Life for Our Time*. London: J. M. Dent, p. 148.

25 Foucault, Michel, 1967, *Madness and Civilization: A History of Insanity in the Age of Reason*, Toronto: New American Library.

26 Demos, John, 1997, "Oedipus and America: Historical Perspectives on the Reception of Psychoanalysis in the United States" and "History and the Psychosocial: Reflections on 'Oedipus and America,'" in J. Pfister and N. Schnog (eds.), *Inventing the Psychological: Toward a Cultural History of Emotional Life in America*, New Haven, CT: Yale University Press, pp. 63–83.

27 Lears, T. J. Jackson, 1994, *No Place of Grace: Antimodernism and the Transformation of American Culture, 1880–1920*, Chicago: Chicago University Press.

28 Kurzweil, Edith, 1998, *The Freudians: A Comparative Perspective*, London: Transaction.

29 Hale, N., 1971, *Freud and the Americans: The Beginnings of Psycho-analysis in the United States*, New York: Oxford University Press; Hale, N., 1995, *The Rise and Crisis of Psychoanalysis in the United States: Freud and the Americans, 1917–1985*, New York: Oxford University Press.

30 Caplan, Eric, 1998, *Mind Games: American Culture and the Birth of Psychotherapy*, Berkeley: University of California Press.

31 See Herman, Ellen, 1995, *The Romance of American Psychology: Political Culture in the Age of Experts*, Berkeley: University of California Press.

32 Ibid.; Cushman, P., 1995, *Constructing the Self, Constructing America: A Cultural History of Psychotherapy*, Boston, MA: Addison-Wesley.

33 Shenhav, Yehuda, 1999, *Manufacturing Rationality*, New York: Oxford University Press, p. 20.

34 Firm owners increasingly pushed away contractors, who until then controlled the production process, and gained control of the workers, of the firing and hiring.

35   Shenhav, *Manufacturing Rationality*.
36   Ibid., p. 206.
37   Ibid.
38   Ibid., p. 197.
39   The infamous Frederick Taylor himself talked about his shock
     at the anger manifested by many factory workers. See Stearns,
     Peter, 1994, *American Cool: Constructing a Twentieth-Century
     Emotional Style*, New York: New York University Press,
     p. 122.
40   Baritz, L., 1979, *Servants of Power: A History of the Use of Social
     Science in American Industry*, Middletown, CT: Wesleyan University Press.
41   Carey, Alex, 1967, "The Hawthorne Studies: A Radical Criticism," *American Sociological Review* 32 (June): 403–16.
42   Susman, Walter, 1984, *Culture as History: The Transformation
     of American Society in the Twentieth Century*, New York:
     Pantheon Books. Susman has documented the passage from
     a "character"-oriented society to a personality-oriented culture.
     He confirms that the emphasis on "personality" had corporate
     origins and that the psychologists' intervention in the cultural
     arena made "personality" something to "play" with, "work on,"
     and manipulate.
43   Mayo, Elton, 1949, *The Social Problems of an Industrial Civilization*, London: Routledge & Kegan Paul, p. 65.
44   Ibid., p. 69.
45   Ibid., p. 72.
46   Stearns, *American Cool*.
47   Coontz, *The Social Origins of Private Life*.
48   Abbott, Andrew, 1988, *The System of Professions: An Essay on
     the Division of Expert Labor*, Chicago: University of Chicago
     Press; Capshew, James H., 1999, *Psychologists on the March:
     Science, Practice, and Professional Identity in America, 1929–
     1969*, Cambridge: Cambridge University Press.
49   Mannheim, Karl, 1936, *Ideology and Utopia*, New York:
     Harcourt Brace Jovanovich, p. 3 (emphasis added).
50   See Kimmel, Michael, 1996, *Manhood in America: A Cultural
     History*, New York: The Free Press
51   Shenhav, *Manufacturing Rationality*, p. 21.
52   Foucault, Michel, 1982, *The Archaeology of Knowledge*, New
     York: Pantheon Books.
53   "The main feature of this 'pragmatist sociology' is to adopt
     (but in very variable proportions) some of the assumptions of
     American pragmatism: the rejection of hypostasis and the

reification of the social phenomena; pluralism; agnosticism; the notion of continuity between everyday-life knowledge and the sociological one (in contrast to the Bachelardian's 'epistemological breaking'). Some watchwords like 'to follow the actors' or 'to observe social phenomena in action' are used as rallying signals by the sociologists of this nebula." Lemieux, Cyril, "New Developments in French Sociology (unpublished manuscript).

54 Dewey, John, 1929, *The Quest for Certainty: A Study of the Relation of Knowledge and Action*, New York: Minton, Balch; Joas, Hans, 1993, *Pragmatism in Social Theory*, Chicago: Chicago University Press; Rawls, Anne Warfield, 1997, "Durkheim and Pragmatism: An Old Twist on a Contemporary Debate," *Sociological Theory* 15(1): 5–29.

55 Fontana, D., 1990, *Social Skills at Work*, Leicester, UK: British Psychological Society, Routledge, p. 23 (author's emphasis).

56 Carnegie, Dale, 1937, *How to Win Friends and Influence People*, New York: Simon and Schuster, p. 218.

57 Margerison, Charles J., 1987, *Conversation Control Skills for Managers*, London: Mercury Books.

58 <http://www.mindtools.com/CommSkll/Communication Intro.htm>

59 See p. 39 in Honneth, Axel (eds.), 2001, "Personal Identity and Disrespect," in S. Seidman and J. Alexander (eds.), *The New Social Theory Reader: Contemporary Debates*, London: Routledge, pp. 39–45.

60 Hocker, Joyce and William Wilmot, 1991, *Interpersonal Conflict*, Dubuque, IA: William C. Brown Publishers, p. 239.

61 <http://www.colorado.edu/conflict/peace/treatment/ commimp.htm>

62 See Brunel, Valerie, "Le 'Developpement Personnel': de la figure du sujet à la figure du pouvoir dans l'organization liberale" (unpublished manuscript).

63 Aubert, Nicole and Vincent de Gaulejac, 1991, *Le Coût de l'Excellence*, Paris: Seuil, p. 148.

64 <http://www.mindtools.com/CommSkll/Communication Intro.htm>

65 Bratich, Jack, Jeremy Packer, and Cameron McCarthy, 2003, *Foucault, Cultural Studies, and Governmentality*, Albany: State University of New York Press.

66 See Elias, Norbert, 2000, *The Civilizing Process*, Oxford, UK: Blackwell Publishing.

67 Fontana, *Social Skills at Work*, p. 8.

68   Cott, Nancy F., 1977, *The Bonds of Womanhood: "Woman's Sphere" in New England, 1780–1835*, New Haven, CT: Yale University Press, p. 231.

69   Ibid.

70   Ibid.

71   Ibid.

72   Schulman, Bruce, 2001, *The Seventies: The Great Shift in American Culture, Society and Politics*, New York: Free Press, p. 171.

73   In 1970 there were less than 20 courses on women in American universities; two decades later, more than 30,000 of such courses were offered at the undergraduate level only. Ibid, p. 172.

74   Berger, John, 1972, *Ways of Seeing*, London: British Broadcasting Corporation, pp. 46–7.

75   "The more I talked to men as well as women, the more it seemed that inner feelings of incompleteness, emptiness, self-doubt, and self-hatred were the same, no matter who experienced them, even if they were expressed in culturally opposite ways." In Steinem, Gloria, 1992, *Revolution From Within: A Book of Self-Esteem*, Boston, MA: Little, Brown & Company, p. 5.

76   Fonda, Jane, 2005, *My Life So Far*, New York: Random House.

77   See D'Emilio, John and Estelle B. Freedman, 1988, *Intimate Matters: A History of Sexuality in America*, New York: Harper and Row.

78   See Shumway, R., 2003, *Modern Love: Romance, Intimacy, and the Marriage Crisis*, New York: New York University Press.

79   Masters, William H. and Johnson, Virginia E. in association with Levin, Robert J., 1974, *The Pleasure Bond: A New Look at Sexuality and Commitment*, Boston, MA: Little, Brown & Company.

80   Ibid., pp. 24–5.

81   Rothman, Ellen, 1984, *Hands and Hearts: A History of Courtship in America*, New York: Basic Books; Lystra, Karen, 1989, *Searching the Heart: Women, Men, and Romantic Love in Nineteenth-Century America*, New York: Oxford University Press.

82   Quoted in Schulman, *The Seventies*, p. 181.

83   Ibid., p. 84.

84   Masters and Johnson in association with Levin, *The Pleasure Bond*, p. 36.

85   Giddens, Anthony, 1992, *The Transformation of Intimacy: Sexuality, Love, and Eroticism in Modern Societies*, Cambridge: Polity.

86   Crain, Mary Beth, "The Marriage Check Up," *Redbook* (unknown date), p. 88.

87   Hendrix, Harville, 1985, "Work at Your Marriage: A Workbook," *Redbook*, October, p. 130.

88   It is important to emphasize, however, that despite the aura of inevitability contained in Weber's analysis, rationalization is not a unilinear process, but is rather replete with tensions and contradictions. This is a point aptly made by Johannes Weiss, "On the Irreversibility of Western Rationalization and Max Weber's Alleged Fatalism," in Lash and Whimster, *Max Weber*, pp. 154–63.

89   Espeland, Wendy N., 2001, "Commensuration and Cognition," in Karen Cerulo (ed.), *Culture in Mind*, New York: Routledge, p. 64.

90   "Mine is an attempt to illustrate where texts, seen as adjuncts of discourse, interpenetrate human action." Stock, Brian, 1990, *Listening for the Text: On the Uses of the Past*, Baltimore and London: Johns Hopkins University Press, pp. 104–5.

91   Goody, J. and I. Watt, 1968, "The Consequences of Literacy," in Jack Goody (ed.), *Literacy in Traditional Societies*, Cambridge: Cambridge University Press, pp. 27–68.

92   Branden, Nathaniel, 1985, "If You Could Hear What I Cannot Say: The Husband/Wife Communication Workshop," *Redbook*, April, p. 94.

93   Gordon, Lori H. and Jon Frandsen, 1993, *Passage to Intimacy: Key Concepts and Skills from the Pairs Program Which Has Helped Thousands of Couples Rekindle Their Love*, New York: Simon & Schuster, p. 114.

94   Ibid., p. 91.

95   Beck, U. and E. Beck-Gernsheim, 1995, *The Normal Chaos of Love*, Cambridge: Polity.

96   Espeland, "Commensuration and Cognition," p. 65.

97   Honneth, "Personal Identity and Disrespect."

98   Habermas, Jürgen, 2001, "Contributions to a Discourse Theory of Law and Democracy," in S. Seidman and J. Alexander (eds.), *The New Social Theory Reader: Contemporary Debates*, London: Routledge, pp. 30–8.

99   Espeland, "Commensuration and Cognition," p. 83.

100   Butler, Judith, 2001, "Can The 'Other' Speak of Philosophy?," in Joan Scott and Debra Keates (eds.), *Schools of Thought: Twenty-Five Years of Interpretive Social Science*, Princeton: Princeton University Press, p. 58.

101   Quoted in Woolard, Kathryn, A., 1998, "Introduction: Language Ideology as a Field of Inquiry," in Bambi B. Schieffelin, Kathryn A. Woolard, and Paul V. Kroskrity (eds.), *Language Ideologies: Practice and Theory*, Oxford: Oxford University Press, p. 4.

Chapter 2 Suffering, Emotional Fields, and Emotional Capital

1   Smiles, Samuel, 1882, *Self-Help*, London: John Murray, p. 6.

2   Ibid., p. 8.

3   Freud, Sigmund, 1919, "Lines of Advance in Psychoanalytic Therapy," *Standard Edition of the Complete Psychological Works*, vol. 17, London: Hogarth Press, pp. 159–68.

4   Quoted in Woody, Melvin J., 2003, "The Unconscious as a Hermeneutic Myth: Defense of the Imagination," in J. Phillips and J. Morley (eds.), *Imagination and Its Pathologies*, Cambridge, MA: MIT Press, p. 191.

5   Brint, Steven, 1990, "Rethinking the Policy Influence of Experts: From General Characterizations to Analysis of Variation," *Sociological Forum* 5(1): 373–5.

6   Rogers, Carl R., 1961, *On Becoming a Person: A Therapist's View of Psychotherapy*, Boston, MA: Houghton Mifflin Company, p. 35.

7   Maslow, Abraham, 1971, *The Farther Reaches of Human Nature*, London: Penguin Books, p. 52.

8   Ibid., p. 57.

9   Reznek, Lawrie, 1991, *The Philosophical Defense of Psychiatry*, New York: Routledge.

10   Botwin, Carol, 1985, "The Big Chill," *Redbook*, February, p. 105.

11   Sewell, William H., 1999, "The Concept(s) of Culture," in Victoria E. Bonnell and Lynn Hunt (eds.), *Beyond the Cultural Turn: New Directions in the Study of Society and Culture*, Berkeley: University of California Press, p. 56.

12   Eagleton, Terry, 1991, *Ideology: An Introduction*, London: Verso, p. 48.

13 Landmark Corporation, <http://www.landmarkeducation. com>

14 Eagleton, *Ideology.*

15 Illouz, Eva, 2003, *Oprah Winfrey and the Glamour of Misery: An Essay on Popular Culture*, New York: Columbia University Press.

16 "Can't Get Over Your Ex," *Redbook*, March 28, 1995.

17 See p. 18 in Gergen, Kenneth J. and Mary Gergen, 1988, "Narrative and the Self as Relationship," in L. Berkowitz (ed.), *Advances in Experimental Social Psychology*, New York: Academic Press, vol. 21, pp. 17–54.

18 Randolph, Laura B., 1993, "Oprah Opens Up About Her Weight, Her Wedding, and Why She Withheld the Book," *Ebony*, October 48(12): 130.

19 Shields, Brooke, 2005, *Down Came the Rain: My Journey Through Postpartum Depression*, New York: Hyperion Press.

20 Fonda, Jane, 2005, *My Life So Far*, New York: Random House.

21 Dowd, Maureen, 2005, "The Roles of a Lifetime," *The New York Times Book Review*, April 24, p. 13.

22 Foucault, Michel, 1994, "Le Souci de Soi," in *Histoire de la Sexualité: le souci de soi*, vol. 3, Paris: Gallimard.

23 Lincoln's remark to John L. Scripps, 1860, Center of the American Constitution. Temporary exhibit on Abraham Lincoln at the National Constitution Center, Philadelphia.

24 Kidron, Carol, 1999, "Amcha's Second Generation Holocaust Survivors: A Recursive Journey into the Past to Construct Wounded Carriers of Memory." Master's thesis, Hebrew University of Jerusalem.

25 Dershowitz, A., 1994, *The Abuse Excuse: And Other Cop-outs, Sob Stories, and Evasions of Responsibility*, Boston, MA: Little, Brown & Co., p. 5.

26 Quoted in Moore, B., 1972, *Reflections on the Causes of Human Misery and Upon Certain Proposals to Eliminate Them*, Boston, MA: Beacon Press, p. 17.

27 Žižek, Slavoj and Glyn Daly, 2004, *Conversations with Žižek*, Cambridge: Polity, p. 141.

28 Meyer, John W., 1986, "The Self and the Life Course: Institutionalization and Its Effects," in A. B. Sørensen, F. E. Weinert, and Lonnie R. Sherrod (eds.), *Human Development and the Life Course: Multidisciplinary Perspectives*, Hillsdale, NJ: LEA, p. 206.

29 DiMaggio, Paul, 1997, "Culture and Cognition," *Annual Review of Sociology* 23: 263–87.

30 Herman, Ellen, 1995, *The Romance of American Psychology: Political Culture in the Age of Experts*, Berkeley: University of California Press, p. 241; an example of such concern in mental health was the fact that some federal agencies such as the Veterans Administration were eager to adopt new programs in mental health.

31 Meyer, John, 1997, "World Society and the Nation State," *American Journal of Sociology* 103(1): 144–81.

32 Miller, Alice, 1981, *The Drama of the Gifted Child*, New York: Basic Books.

33 Miller, Alice, 1990, *Banished Knowledge: Facing Childhood Injuries*, New York: Anchor Books.

34 Micale, Mark S. and Paul Lerner (eds.), 2001, *Traumatic Pasts: History, Psychiatry, and Trauma in the Modern Age, 1870–1930*. New York: Cambridge University Press, p. 2.

35 Ibid., p. 261.

36 Ibid., p. 12.

37 Kutchins, Herb and Stuart A. Kirk, 1997, *Making Us Crazy: DSM: The Psychiatric Bible and the Creation of Mental Disorders*, New York: The Free Press, p. 17.

38 *Diagnostic and Statistical Manual of Mental Disorders (DSM III)*, 1980, 3rd edn, Washington, DC: American Psychiatric Association, p. 63.

39 Ibid., p. 313.

40 Ibid., p. 323.

41 Kutchins and Kirk, *Making Us Crazy*, p. 247. Much of the discussion of the DSM is based on this book. Some claim that some pharmaceutical companies even directly contributed to the development of the DSM.

42 Ibid., p. 13.

43 An example of their study is how the hygienists supported Pasteur's theories of microbes because this could provide a justification for their fight against insalubrious accommodations. Latour, Bruno, 1988, *The Pasteurization of France*, Cambridge, MA: Harvard University Press; Callon, Michel, 1986, "Some Elements of a Sociology of Translation," in John Law (ed.), *Power, Action and Belief*, London: Routledge & Kegan Paul, pp. 196–233.

44 Foucault, Michel, 1990, *The History of Sexuality: An Introduction*, New York: Vintage, p. 71.

45 See p. 488 in Schweder, Richard A., 1988, "Suffering in Style," *Culture, Medicine and Psychiatry* 12(4): 479–97.

46 Bourdieu, Pierre and Loïc Wacquant, 1992, *An Invitation to Reflexive Sociology*, Chicago: University of Chicago Press.

47 Bourdieu, Pierre, 1979, *La Distinction: Critique sociale du jugement*, Paris: Editions de Minuit.

48 See p. 243 in Bourdieu, Pierre, 1986, "The Forms of Capital," in John G. Richardson (ed.), *Handbook of Theory and Research for the Sociology of Education*, New York: Greenwood Press, pp. 241–58.

49 Walsh, Bruce and Nancy Betz, 1985, *Tests and Assessments*, Englewood Cliffs, NJ: Prentice Hall, p. 110.

50 See p. 433 in Mayer, J. D. and P. Salovey, 1993, "The Intelligence of Emotional Intelligence," *Intelligence* 17: 433–42; see also Salovey, Peter and John D. Mayer, 1990, "Emotional Intelligence," *Imagination, Cognition, and Personality* 9: 185–211.

51 Fass, Paula S., 1980, "The IQ: A Cultural and Historical Framework," *American Journal of Education* 4: 431–58.

52 Cherniss, Cary, "The Business Case for Emotional Intelligence" <http://www.eiconsortium.org/research/business_case_for_ei.htm>

53 <http://www.managementconnection.com/resilience_ei_business_case.html>

54 To the extent however that cultural capital, at least in the Bourdieusian sense, means access to an established corpus of artistic creations identified as "high culture," emotional intelligence does not qualify as a subspecies of cultural capital.

55 Portes, Alejandro, 1998, "Social Capital: Its Origins and Applications in Modern Sociology," *Annual Review of Sociology* 24: 1–24.

56 Boltanski, Luc and Eve Chapiello, 1999, *Le Nouvel Esprit du Capitalisme*, Paris: Gallimard, p. 176.

57 Walzer, Michael, 1983, *Spheres of Justice: A Defense of Pluralism and Equality*, Oxford: Martin Robertson.

58 Sennett, Richard, 1998, *The Corrosion of Character: The Personal Consequences of Work in the New Capitalism*, New York and London: Norton, p. 117.

59 Freud, S., 1963, "Introductory Lectures on Psychoanalysis, Part III," in J. Strachey (ed.), *The Standard Edition of the Complete Psychological Works of Sigmund Freud*, London: Hogarth Press, pp. 352–3.

60   Beck, Ulrich, 1995, *The Normal Chaos of* Love, Cambridge: Polity.

Chapter 3 Romantic Webs

*   This lecture was written in collaboration with Nick John.
1   See p. 187 in Merkle, Erich R. and Rhonda A. Richardson, 2000, "Digital Dating and Virtual Relating: Conceptualizing Computer Mediated Romantic Relationships," *Family Relations* 49: 187–92.
2   See p. 100 in Lupton, Deborah, 1995, "The Embodied Computer/User," in Mike Featherstone and Roger Burrows (eds.), *Cyberspace, Cyberbodies, Cyberpunk: Cultures of Technological Embodiment*, London: Sage, pp. 97–112.
3   Stoughton, Stephanie, 2001, "Log on, Find Love," *The Boston Globe*, February 11.
4   Today, match.com's website claims that 89,000 people have found the love of their life via their site, and that they have more than 12 million posted users in 246 countries using 18 different languages. Rival site matchnet.com claims to have 9.5 million active members.
5   Brooks, David, 2003, "Love, Internet Style," *New York Times*, November 8; Wexler, Kathryn, 2004, "Dating Websites Get More Personal," *The Miami Herald*, January 20.
6   Saillart, Catherine, 2004, "Internet Dating Goes Gray," *LA Times*, May 19.
7   Davies, Jennifer, 2002, "Cupid's Clicks," *San Diego Union Tribune*, February 10.
8   I interviewed approximately 15 Israelis and 10 Americans for the purpose of this research. Although there are obvious cultural differences between the two samples, I was struck by the extraordinary convergence in the use and meaning of Internet dating sites.
9   Silverstein, Judith and Michael Lasky, 2004, *Online Dating for Dummies*, New York: Wiley, p. 109.
10   Ben-Zeev, Aharon, 2004, *Love Online: Emotions on the Internet*, Cambridge: Cambridge University Press.
11   Quoted in Shusterman, Richard, 2000, *Performing Live: Aesthetic Alternatives for the Ends of Art*, Ithaca, NY: Cornell University Press, p. 154.

12 Katz, Evan Marc, 2003, *I Can't Believe I'm Buying This Book: A Commonsense Guide to Successful Internet Dating*, Berkeley, CA: Ten Speed Press, p. 96.

13 Lukács, György, 1971, *History and Class Consciousness: Studies in Marxist Dialectics*, Cambridge, MA: MIT Press, p. 83.

14 Katz, *I Can't Believe I'm Buying This Book*, p. 108.

15 Agger, Ben, 2004, *Speeding up Fast Capitalism: Cultures, Jobs, Families, Schools, Bodies*, Boulder, CO: Paradigm, pp. 1–5.

16 Katz, *I Can't Believe I'm Buying This Book*, p. 103.

17 Žižek, Slavoj, 1989, *The Sublime Object of Ideology*, Verso: London, p. 32.

18 Schurmans, Marie-Noëlle and Loraine Dominicé, 1997, *Le Coup de Foudre Amoureux: essai de sociologie compréhensive*, Paris: Presses Universitaires de France.

19 The following pages on critique follow closely or are direct quotations from chapter 8 of my book, *Oprah Winfrey and the Glamour of Misery*, 2003, New York: Columbia University Press.

20 Salusinszky, I. and J. Derrida, 1987, *Criticism in Society: Interviews with Jacques Derrida, Northrop Frye, Harold Bloom, Geoffrey Hartman, Frank Kermode, Edward Said, Barbara Johnson, Frank Lentricchia, and Hillis Miller*, New York: Methuen, p. 159.

21 To give one example among many: at the turn of the century capitalists worried about meeting increasing consumer demands hired women at wages that were far lower than those of their male counterparts. This blunt economic inequality provided a great impetus for the feminist movement. See Hobsbawm, Eric J., 1987, *The Age of the Empire, 1875–1914*, New York: Pantheon Books.

22 This is Nussbaum's view in her argument with Dworkin and McKinnon. See "Objectification," in Nussbaum, Martha C., 1999, *Sex and Social Justice*, New York: Oxford University Press. The article "Objectification" previously appeared as Martha C. Nussbaum, 1995, "Objectification," *Philosophy and Public Affairs* 24(4): 249–91.

23 Held, D., 1980, *Introduction to Critical Theory: Horkheimer to Habermas*. Berkeley: University of California Press, pp. 183–4.

24 Walzer, M., 1983, *Spheres of Justice*, New York: Basic Books.

25 Walzer, M., 1988, *The Company of Critics: Social Criticism in the Twentieth Century*, London: Peter Halban.

26 Walzer, M., 1987, *Interpretation and Social Criticism*, Cambridge, MA: Harvard University Press.

27   Latour, Bruno, 1988, *The Pasteurization of France*, Cambridge, MA: Harvard University Press; Callon, Michel, 1986, "Some Elements of a Sociology of Education," in John Law (ed.), *Power, Action and Belief*, London: Routledge & Kegan Paul, pp. 196–233.
28   Silverstein and Lasky, *Online Dating for Dummies*, p. 227.
29   Ibid.
30   Habermas, Jürgen, 1990, *Moral Consciousness and Communicative Action*, Cambridge: Polity.
31   As Koselleck puts it: "My thesis is that in modern times the difference between experience and expectation has increasingly expanded; more precisely, that modernity is first understood as a new age from the time that expectations have distanced themselves evermore from all previous experience" (in Habermas, *Moral Consciousness*, p. 12).
32   Wilson, Timothy D., 2002, *Strangers to Ourselves: Discovering the Adaptive Unconscious*, Cambridge, MA: Belknap Press, p. 73.
33   Goffman, Erving, 1963, *Behavior in Public Places: Notes on the Social Organization of Gatherings*, New York: The Free Press, p. 17.
34   Katz, *I Can't Believe I'm Buying This Book*, p. 105.
35   Hatfield, Elaine and Susan Sprecher, 1986, *Mirror, Mirror: The Importance of Looks in Everyday Life*, Albany: State University of New York Press, p. 118.
36   Ibid., p. 119.
37   Bourdieu, Pierre and Loïc Wacquant, 1992, *An Invitation to Reflexive Sociology*, Chicago: University of Chicago Press, p. 172.
38   Person, Ethel Spector, 1988, *Dreams of Love and Fateful Encounters: the Power of Romantic Passion*, New York: Norton, p. 43.
39   Ibid., p. 114.
40   Mitchell, Stephen A., 2003, *Can Love Last? The Fate of Romance Over Time*, New York: Norton, pp. 95, 104.
41   Edgar, Howard Brian and Howard Martin Edgar, 2003, *The Ultimate Man's Guide to Internet Dating: the Premier Men's Resource for Finding, Attracting, Meeting, and Dating Women Online*, Aliso Viejo, CA: Purple Bus, p. 12.
42   Welton, Donn, 1999, "Soft, Smooth Hands: Husserl's Phenomenology of the Lived Body," in Donn Welton (ed.), *The Body: Classic and Contemporary Readings*. Malden, MA: Blackwell, pp. 38–56.
43   Ibid., p. 45.
44   Schooler, Jonathan W., Stella Ohlsson, and Kevin Brooks, 1993, "Thoughts Beyond Words: When Language Overshadows Insight," *Journal of Experimental Psychology* 122(2):166–83.

45 See Iyengar, Sheena and Mark R. Lepper, 2000, "When Choice is Demotivating: Can One Desire Too Much of a Good Thing?", *Journal of Personality and Social Psychology* 79(6): 995–1006; Klein, G., 1998, *Sources of Power: How People Make Decisions*, Cambridge, MA: MIT Press; Wilson, Timothy D. and Jonathan W. Schooler, 1991, "Thinking Too Much: Introspection can Reduce the Quality of Preferences and Decisions," *Journal of Personality and Social Psychology* 60(2): 181–92; Schooler et al., "Thoughts Beyond Words"; Schwartz, Barry, 2000, "Self-Determination: The Tyranny of Freedom," *American Psychologist* 55(1): 79–88; Schwartz, Barry, Andrew Ward, John Monterosso, Sonja Lyubomirsky, Katherine White and Darrin R. Lehman, 2002, "Maximising Versus Satisfying: Happiness is a Matter of Choice," *Journal of Personality and Social Psychology* 83(5): 1178–97.

46 Wilson and Schooler, "Thinking Too Much."

47 When John Updike says that "An imagined kiss is more easily controlled, more thoroughly enjoyed, and less cluttery than an actual kiss," he is referring to an act of imagination, grounded in experience, that is, with someone one has actually met (quoted on p. 31 in John Updike, 2004, "Libido Lite," in *The New York Review of Books*, November 18, pp. 30–1).

48 See Phillips, James and James Morley (eds.), 2003, *Imagination and Its Pathologies*, Cambridge, MA: MIT Press, pp. 191, 10.

49 McKenna, Katelyn Y. A., Arnies Green, and Marci Gleason, 2002, "Relationship Formation on the Internet: What's the Big Attraction?" *Journal of Social Issues* 58(1): 9–31.

50 For a superlative work on the intertwining of money and sentiments, see Viviana Zelizer, 2005, *The Purchase of Intimacy*, Princeton, NJ: Princeton University Press.

51 See p. 128 in Eva Illouz, 1999, "That Shadowy Realm of Interior: Oprah Winfrey and Hamlet's Glass," *International Journal of Cultural Studies* 2(1): 109–31.

52 Arditi, Jorge, 1996, "Simmel's Theory of Alienation and the Decline of the Nonrational," *Social Theory* 14(2): 93–108.

53 Damasio, Antonio R., 1994, *Descartes' Error: Emotion, Reason, and the Human Brain*, New York: Putnam Publishing Group, pp. 193–4.

54 Žižek, Slavoj and Glyn Daly, 2004, *Conversations with Žižek*, Cambridge: Polity, p. 111.

Index